MW00565238

Steven Holl

Edited by
Francesco Garofalo

Universe

First published in the United States of America in 2003
by UNIVERSE PUBLISHING
A Division of Rizzoli International Publications, Inc.
300 Park Avenue South
New York, NY 10010
www. Rizzoliusa.com

Editorial design and book packaging:
Colophon srl, Venice, Italy

Editorial Coordinator: Maria Giulia Montessori

Translation: Christopher Huw Evans

Special thanks to Aislinn Weidele

2003 2004 2005 2006 2007/ 10 9 8 7 6 5 4 3 2 1

Printed in Italy

ISBN: 0-7893-1006-6

Library of Congress Catalog Control Number: 2003104962

Contents

YET ANOTHER MONOGRAPH?
FRANCESCO GAROFALO

This book on Steven Holl belongs to a tradition of compact monographs that has perhaps not yet received the appreciation it deserves. Commencing with the two books on Le Corbusier and Mies van der Rohe published by Artemis of Zurich many years ago, generations of architects and above all students, have taken advantage of them to make their first contact with those whom we are accustomed to call the "masters." Besides, not everyone can afford to buy the *Oeuvre Complète* in their first year at university, or are willing to confine themselves to skimming through it in the library. Since those two models from just after the war, many European publishing houses including Zanichelli in Italy, Gustavo Gili in Spain, and Birkhäuser in Switzerland have produced successful series of volumes, sometimes exchanging translations.

The characteristics of this literary genre, looked down on by historians, are fairly constant. A series of projects grouped by themes or in chronological order; an appearance of objectivity which sometimes conceals a tendentious interpretation; an author who necessarily remains in the background with respect to the subject of the book. Equally evident are the limitations of small monographs: in the first instance, the reduction of a great architect's complexity to a brief succession of projects and built works.

Thus the editing of a book like this has become an ever more difficult task, in part because some of the best architects are nowadays involved in the definition of their own critical standing as the authors of special creative and intellectual autobiographies. It is therefore the responsibility of the introduction to recount, at least in part, what had to be left out of the book owing to the demands and aforementioned limitations of the formula.

In Steven Holl's case there is a great deal that is not to be found in this book and that can be used to hint, through his role, at just what it is that makes a modern architect different from a contemporary architect. It is precisely the complexity of his interests that makes it worth examining this distinction from a historical perspective. There have been other figures in architecture versatile and creative enough to have been able to carry out a great number of activities in addition to the customary ones: from criticism to publishing, from industrial design to the design of furniture, etc. Gio Ponti is an excellent example. For Steven Holl, the ambition is to equal this range, but to do so in the depth of his thinking, which is closely bound up with the conception of his work.

If the "manifesto" was the most typical expression of modern architecture, what characterizes contemporary architecture is the production of theory. Instead of a few, incontrovertible statements, a continual probing of key concepts, in which the separateness of architecture as a discipline is brought into question by comparison with other forms of critical and philosophical thought. In contrast to the two possible schemes inherited from modernity—first the declarations of principle and then the works or, vice versa, a series of principles deduced by the critics from a corpus of architecture—Steven Holl has linked research and design in a way that brings him close to the figures who have most characterized late twentieth-century architecture, from Aldo Rossi to Rem Koolhaas.

Steven Holl's activity took on a new and powerful impetus in the second half of the nineties. Even though this book seeks to put a career spanning twenty-five years into broad and balanced perspective, the need to reflect the current state of his research has obliged us to make some difficult choices in selecting his projects. Hence it is more useful to reconstruct his evolution through some of the themes that characterize, without differentiating, his professional projects and his experimental research, given that both contribute to intensify the experience of his architecture.

The next few paragraphs will examine Steven Holl's books and publications as vehicles of research. They will be followed by his sketches and drawings, and then by his relationship with the tradition of the American house, which had such an influence at the beginning of his career. His urban visions, on a scale that is only today starting to take on the potential of concrete projects, already contained in the eighties the germs of those environmental preoccupations that characterize his most recent projects. And finally an attempt will be made to describe the shift from "typology" to "topology" that released the form of his architecture from the shackles of the modern. In this last passage it becomes evident how each project is associated with the recourse to a "limited concept" which the architect uses as a sort of defense mechanism against the opposing siren calls of arbitrariness and *a priori* stylistic consistency.

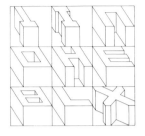

Covers of "Pamphlet Architecture", nos. 5, 7 and 9.

The relationship with theory: a sequence of books

The first volume in the series *Pamphlet Architecture* came out in 1977 in a limited edition of just one hundred copies. Over the following years, the series maintained the character of a flexible instrument open to a variety of authors and themes in keeping with the interests of Steven Holl and his closest collaborators. They are small-scale publications, even in their format, and are intended to serve as a documentation of research, rather than as a mere means of promotion. Holl prepared some of the first issues: *Bridges* (1), *The Alphabetical City* (5), *Bridge of Houses* (7), *Urban and Rural House Types* (9) and, with J. Fenton, *Hybrid Buildings* (11). The typological approach is clear from the titles. But it is a nonsystematic typology, remote from the classical taxonomy of modernism, and to some extent from the Italian and European research of the previous decade. The investigation makes use of essential drawings, almost exclusively based on the apparent objectivity of axonometrics. In this way, urban buildings are analyzed for their formal properties: the extrusion of their footprints resembling letters of the alphabet. The *Bridge Of Houses* and *Hybrid Buildings* opened the way to themes that are investigated further in the projects, which weave concrete observations and literary suggestions. Learning from the phenomena of hybridization and the unplanned mixing of functions has helped the architect to break down the determinism of typological rules.

Anchoring was the first collection of his projects published by Princeton Architectural Press in 1988. The book design is indicative of the ambition to present Steven Holl as the heir to an interrupted tradition of European architects. The square format, cloth binding and Helvetica typeface echo the publishing formulas of the period between the two wars. Kevin Lippert—the publisher—wrote an unusual introduction which, beyond giving a thorough interpretation of Holl's work, places him in an equidistant position between the rush for commercial success of so many professionals and the intellectualist attitudes of the East Coast. Even before Steven Holl himself gets around to doing it, Lippert seeks to clarify the meaning of the title, which is metaphorical rather than literal: anchoring to the site. The projects might suggest a neo-modernist and typological approach, but this is transcended in the author's text-cum-manifesto. Some of the key terms in the evolution of his theory are already explained in this writing, which starts with the declaration: "Architecture is bound to situation." (S. Holl, "Anchoring," in *idem, Anchoring*, Princeton Architectural Press, New York 1989, p. 9).

Here the "limited concept" made its appearance as an alternative to ideology. Today this latter word has assumed a negative connotation, but in the eighties it could still be seen as a legitimate polemical target. It is regarded almost as a system of rigid rules which Holl preferred to dispense with, but which he felt obliged to replace with an intellectual framework of his own, offered as a premise to the work he had already done, and to the experimental nature of his work in the future.

Intertwining, published in 1996, constituted a companion to the preceding volume. The introduction needed to explain an apparent contradiction. The mainly theoretical work of the first book had been greatly extended on the professional plane. It no longer seemed particularly "anchored," and indeed appeared to have been internationalized by projects located in Japan, Finland, Germany, Switzerland, the Netherlands, Korea, and Norway.

The book introduced the new central interest in Steven Holl's thinking, an interpretation of phenomenology based primarily on the reading of Maurice Merleau-Ponty and his *Phenomenology of Perception*. With the task of linking the philosophical references to the technical and historical scenario of contemporary architecture entrusted to Alberto Perez Gomez, the architect expounded his own design program based on "intertwining." The discourse unfolds through a heterogeneous series of terms. Sometimes these are keywords like "enmeshing," at others, statements such as "perception is metaphorical," "time is duration," or metaphors like that of the stone and the feather. However, the conclusion

Covers of the volumes Anchoring, Intertwining *and* Parallax.

9

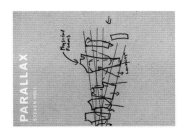

of the text, the section "remaining experimental," confirms the primacy of an experience that can only be provided by architecture: "Our aim is to realize space with strong phenomenal properties while elevating architecture to a level of thought." (S. Holl, "Intertwining," in *idem*, *Intertwining*, Princeton Architectural Press, New York 1996, p. 16).

The title of *Parallax*, published in 2000, already suggests that a new scientific dimension has been grafted onto the two previous ones (typological and phenomenological), lending them new force. The illustrations are almost all taken from the storehouse of the sciences, and in particular the new science of complexity. Though *Parallax* is a different kind of book. It is no longer a catalogue of projects, nor is it just a series of meditations. Steven Holl does not feel the need to remain within the bounds of the monograph, in which the uniqueness of his work is allowed to emerge against the conventional backdrop of the format. His reflections are now methodically interwoven with the projects in a continuous flow. This is all the more unusual because he is moving in the opposite direction to that of the majority of architects, whose professional success prevents them from maintaining the continuity of their theoretical research, favoring the production of "complete works" in installments.

In the "Acknowledgments" he declares: "This book affirms a spirit in architecture and discoveries in science and perception, and tries to explore the relation of one to the other." (S. Holl, "Acknowledgments," in *idem*, *Parallax*, Princeton Architectural Press, New York 2000, p. 9). This may provide a clue to the more evident formal complexity of his recent projects, developed since the beginning of the new millennium. The last publication in which Steven Holl has been involved represents in some way a return to *Pamphlet Architecture*. It is a magazine called *32*, produced between New York and Beijing. It is not then a personal vehicle but a group endeavor. With this choice he is undermining the image of the New York intellectual inhabiting an island somewhere between Europe and America, establishing a thematic and geographical horizon more in keeping with our time. It is a way of raising cultural and political, as well as disciplinary questions, and of balancing the agnosticism that professional practice allows to slip in behind the most virtuous discourses on the autonomy of architecture.

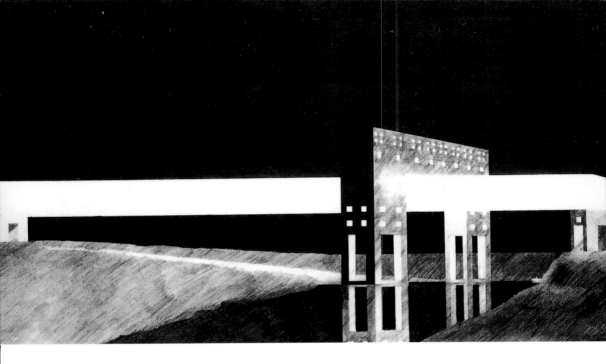

Written in Water

Continuity and evolution also characterize Steven Holl's relationship with drawing and painting. His output of watercolors has attained such a dimension and organic unity that the volume in which they are collected, with the evocative title *Written in Water*, is several centimeters thick. At the beginning his drawings were in pencil, from the view of the project for Manila that opens *Anchoring*, to the house in Cleveland at the end of the eighties. The technique of these drawings was fairly different from the one he now uses, as was their function. At a time when few of his works had been constructed, axonometric projections and above all perspective drawings were assigned the task of describing the project and the context. Consistently with the rigorous and rather abrasive character of his architectural vocabulary, these views were steeped in a fairly somber atmosphere, often illuminated by moonlight against a black background. The shift to watercolor has ushered in a new use of representation. The sequence of sketches has become a genuine laboratory in which the genesis, the development of alternatives and the strategy of communication are all closely linked. The drawing appears to be, as the conclusions will attempt to explain, the principal means of control chosen by the architect in order to handle the complexity of his own production.

Gimnasium Bridge, South Bronx, New York 1977.

11

*Sarphatistraat
Offices, Amsterdam,
Netherlands
1996-2000,
watercolor.*

As one sees, the sketches often have the elaborate construction of small three-dimensional views. In many cases they serve as a guide for subsequent computer renderings produced by his studio. It is not just the traditional concept sketch that is affected, but the whole descriptive sequence of the project.

One factor has been crucial in the adoption of this technique: "Watercolor allows you to make bodies of light, to go from the bright to the dark." (A. Zaera Polo, "A Conversation with Steven Holl," in *El Croquis*, 78, 2000, *Steven Holl 1986-1996*, p. 19). The effects created by light are then subjected to verification with models and finally on the computer. A similar process takes place with the keywords and concepts identified for each project, and transcribed on the paper. With the passage of time these drawings have acquired an essential place on the pages of all his publications. It can be said that there is not a single design, whether realized or not, that has not been accompanied by a selection of watercolors. By this means the

architect seems to want to reassure us about its "authenticity" and its correspondence to the concept, and thus of his capacity to predict in abstract the perceptual and phenomenological effects of his works of architecture. The special quality of the sketchbook pages can best be appreciated in exhibitions, for which they are set free from the homogeneity of the reproduction on glossy paper and brought back in scale with plans and models. For the exhibition which accompanied the publication of *Parallax* in 2000-01, an unbroken strip of watercolors wound its way along the walls of the rooms. In recent years Steven Holl's technique has undergone further evolution, with the creation of hybrid images: combinations of painting, photography and computer rendering through collage. These representations reflect the diversity of his imagination, blending the "natural" ingredient of his own drawing and painting with the anonymous and "artificial" digital one, as used in the projects for Toolenburg-Zuid in the Netherlands and for New Nanning in China.

Competition project for the Toolenburg-Zuid housing complex, Schiphol, Netherlands 2001-2002, watercolor.

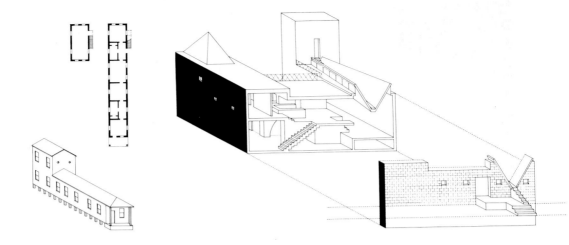

Vernacular American Tradition

Left, schemes
of Camel-Back
Shotgun House,
New Orleans.

Right, Metz House,
Staten Island,
New York 1980.

"In *Urban and Rural House Types* we analyzed the minimum basic house forms as they developed in vernacular architecture in America. We discovered strange and amazingly repeated aspects. Deep mysteries of architecture were revealed in very humble houses." (J. Pallasmaa, "Thought, Matter and Experience [a conversation with Steven Holl]," in *El Croquis*, 108, 2002, *Steven Holl 1998-2002*, p. 24).

The houses designed by Steven Holl can be placed in two families that partly succeed one another in time, and partly overlap. The common feature of the first group is a relationship with the American vernacular tradition. The second derives more directly from those "limited concepts" that have become the mainspring of his research.

In the first phase of his work, the theme of the house is already presented as a mixture. However important the references to traditional typologies may be, they are combined with and adapted to the requirements imposed by the client and by the evocative and literary impulses of the designer. The Telescope House of 1978 is directly inspired by 18th-century precedents on the Atlantic coast. The Metz House of 1980 reworks a patio model, giving it an introverted and urban character and reflecting in forms and materials the complementary nature of the clients: an artist couple—she a painter and he a sculptor. In the Van Zandt House of 1983 another traditional example is cited, the dog-trot house, but it is split in two and reconnected by a swimming pool, with the surreal effect of reproducing the route between the two constructions in the coming and going of the pools.

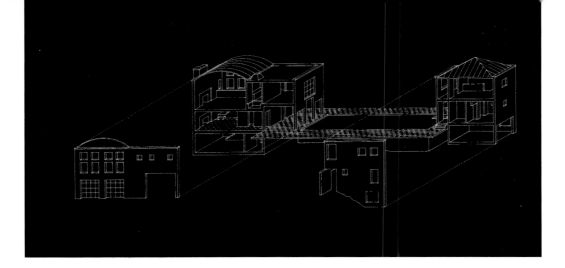

The archetype of the Berkowitz-Odgis House can be found in *Pamphlet Architecture* no. 9, the camel-back shotgun house. Beginning with this reference, other images are grafted onto the design of the house, such as the skeleton of a whale evoked by Melville, which leads Holl to put the wooden frame on the outside instead of the inside, and the "Widows Walk" inspired by the porch where fishermen's wives awaited the return of their husbands on the Atlantic Coast.

Van Zandt House, East Hampton, New York 1983.

If the house on Martha's Vineyard is the most mature result of this first cycle of projects, the red Y House seems to return to some of its themes ten years later. The isolated American house in the landscape is always an apparently fragile object, its structure barely protected by a homogeneous skin. As such it seems to challenge the boundless space of the wilderness. The use of asphalt and stone is carefully avoided in the access to these buildings. The land extending to the edge of the raised platform and point-like foundations, characteristic of these systems of construction, is a way of underlining their heroic solitude. To this feature, the Y House adds the peculiarity of a scheme inspired by the dowsing rod of the water diviner and by the mythical evocation of rooting in the ground. Although this has never been stated explicitly, it is possible to see in it a sort of American translation of the Casa Malaparte on Capri. Moreover, this building rooted in the rock, painted red, and with its roof sloping to the ground, is one of the few cited by Holl in the introduction to *Anchoring*.

Urban mega-forms

Steven Holl's understanding of the scale and form of the city and his initial interest in typology bring him close to those positions in European culture that reaffirmed the primacy of urban architecture in the seventies and eighties. Yet from the outset, his projects have contained an uncanny element, an attempt to renegotiate, rather than subvert, the rules of the city.

His 1985 building at Seaside respects the layout of the hexagonal plaza and integrates the porch and the facade, avoiding a contrast with the eclectic confusion of the context. However, in the very definition of hybrid building, he announces a combination of unusual spaces and functions, commencing with the courtyard between the tower-houses set on the roof of the commercial base. At Fukuoka he begins with a comb-shaped plan, which is part of the typological catalogue of modernism. The serial nature of the apartments is then deformed by the search for an individual character that draws its inspiration from Japanese culture. At Makuhari, finally, the large urban block is called into question through a twofold strategy. The perimeter is opened up and inflected in such a way that the separate fragments acquire a character of their own and the figure of the plan suggests an ideogram. However, the disposition is not arbitrary, but determined by the study of the shadows cast by the tall volumes. A second strategy consists of a contrast to the large and "silent" blocks provided by pavilions and thematic houses that establish a bridge with images and concepts of the local culture, in an indirect and rarefied manner.

At the end of the eighties, a series of experimental projects revealed the emergence of new ideas and sensibilities in Steven Holl's production. It seems as if his individual buildings took on a new, more totemic and idiosyncratic character from these projects onward. But the crucial design for this new interpretation of urban space is the one developed for the exhibition at the 1987 Milan Triennale. Even though the program is invented and constructed out of a mixture of utopian and sentimental ideas (such as the hotel for unhappy lovers), the observations on the city are very clear-cut. The design is the fruit of a precise theoretical program that presents a polemical challenge to those Italian architects who are continuing the tradition of urban studies. In a small sketch published in *Anchoring* we find

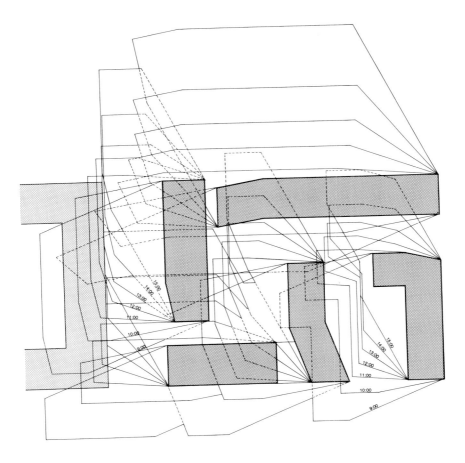

Makurari Housing, Chiba, Japan 1992-96. Shadow diagram.

Porta Vittoria,
Milan 1986.
Concept sketch:
"From perspective
to space."

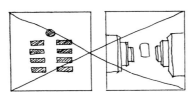

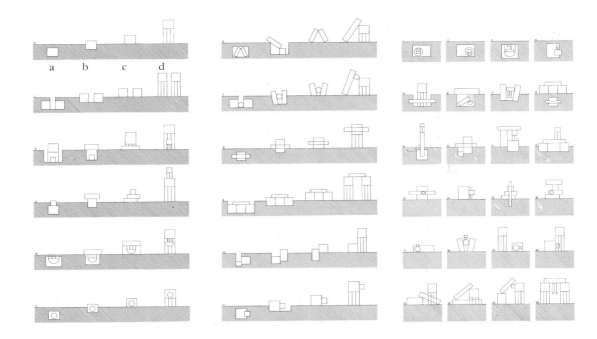

a b c d

18

Correlational charts.

A table of links and correlations beginning with the four conditions of architecture:

A under the ground

B in the ground

C on the ground

D over the ground

On the right, the first two columns: primary relations.

On the left, the third column: complex relations.

a perspective composition that is reminiscent of one of Aldo Rossi's "parti." An X is traced on it, and this is contrasted with another scheme in which the buildings are set on a plane in an apparently haphazard manner and determine a labyrinthine and accidental perspective.

The variations in program are too intense in the contemporary city to rely solely on the stability of urban forms: "Three traditional urban strategies were rejected. The flexible planning device of the grid was suspended, because of its tendency to render everything as a measure of block-by-block infill. Secondly, the method that organizes historically modeled building types according to the existing morphology of the city was suspended. Finally, the whole method of drawing a plan layout, followed later by a three-dimensional form, was rejected." (S. Holl, "Porta Vittoria Milan, Italy 1986," in *Anchoring,* cit., p. 97).

This conclusion has made the project for Porta Vittoria a point of reference for many subsequent works, and the "correlational chart" that accompanies it is one of Steven Holl's most important drawings: a sort of architectural program that was to be developed over the following years.

The notions of density and rarefaction also lie at the base of the theoretical projects collected under the title *Edge of a City.* The sprawl of the suburbs has brought with it the expansion of the network of freeways. The distance from urban centers generates other centers, but ones in which the density and mixture of functions characteristic of major centers are not reproduced. This situation has thrown into crisis, through standardization, cities that have different layouts, and indiscriminately consumes landscapes that are equally diverse. The response of the projects assumes configurations provocatively based on diversity, taking its cue precisely from the urban form and the specific landscape of each of the examples.

In the case of Cleveland he traces Xs, at whose intersection the density of the city increases only to pass suddenly to the rarefaction of the countryside. At Phoenix, the "spatial retaining bars" define a line of transition with the desert. At Forth Worth the "spiroid sectors" mark the angles of large expanses of prairie. This space, which once surrounded the settlement and stretched all the way to the horizon, is now cut out like a planimetric figure in a defensive strategy. The proposals investigate the possibilities of order created by the repetition and variation of a building taken to its extreme consequences. The building components are not very large, but are multiplied to be used as the instrument of an urban strategy. It is interesting to note that in all the publications the accurately drawn plans of the cities are necessarily reproduced on such a small scale that the proposed buildings are practically invisible. Vice versa, the photomontages present the models in scale with the landscape, evoking Corbusian images. Their meaning, however, is inverted because the abstraction of the architectural forms does not derive from a repeatable functional prototype, but is inevitably linked to the character of each city.

In the nineties, a concern for the environment and not just for urbanism, emerged as an additional theme in Steven Holl's work. On the one hand he has taken a public stance in criticizing the American government's attitude to the Kyoto protocol; on the other he has striven to bring into his projects, systems and principles of environmental compatibility and energy conservation, along with solutions derived from natural phenomena. Examples include the house on Kauai, an ocean refuge on the most remote of the Hawaiian Islands, and the facades of the Massachusetts Institute of Technology dormitory, in which the depth of the openings is designed to have an effect on the exposure to sunlight and on the comfort of the occupants.

The most interesting application of this attitude is to be found in a project that represents one of this architect's rare incursions into the field of landscape design. A considerable part of the park currently being laid out at Lake Whitney is set above a water treatment plant. Here he was able to combine his scientific interests with the technique of conceptual elaboration around an environmental theme. From "micro to macro," the geometric sectors into which the park is divided, are inspired by the processes of purification that are carried out on the level below. The small building component makes its way above the park like a drop of water elongated into an organic form faced with steel. However mechanical, certain transpositions may appear, the program is handled in such a way that the different water states are able to intensify the experience of the vegetation and the outdoor space. The same thing happens—but in this case regarding the surfaces and spaces of the building—in the extension to the Cranbrook Institute of Science.

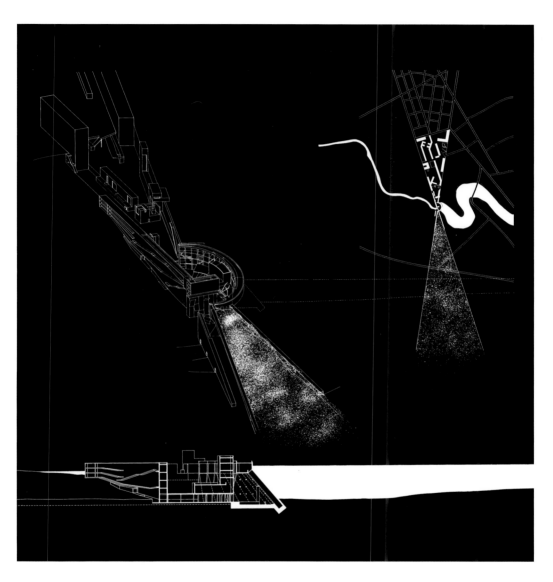

Stitch Plan, Cleveland, Ohio, 1989, axonometric projection of hybrid dam,
site plan and building section.

Diagrams and Concepts

Steven Holl used an autobiographical anecdote to explain the shift that has taken place in his vision of architecture from typology to topology: "In the 1980s I published little manifestoes in the *Pamphlet Architecture* series. In two issues ... I argued for reconstructing the city by stark interpretations of type, a zero ground of architecture. In 1984, on a long train ride across Canada, a philosophy student introduced me to the work of Maurice Merleau-Ponty. ... With the reflective capacities of phenomenology, an intrinsic understanding of space, and a pure passage from the sign to the signified, it is possible to move from the particular to the universal. The seer and the architectural space were no longer opposites; the horizon includes the seer. A new topological openness in the form of a field that extends to a "horizon-structure" became my theoretical frame (no longer simple morphology-typology)." (S. Holl, *Parallax*, cit., p. 302). The period of elaboration that accompanied this discovery lasted exactly a decade, until the publication of *Questions of Perception* in 1994 (with contributions by A. Perez Gomez and J. Pallasmaa). The essay, divided into areas of phenomena, presents experience, including those less commonly identified with architecture such as sound and circumstance, as a basis of opportunity waiting to be catalyzed by special concepts.

The Stretto House offers excellent possibilities for a verification of these ideas, inasmuch as it is a work of transition. The site, crossed by a stream, is divided by a series of small concrete dams. The house, which is set on sloping ground, is also structured by small dams, rectangular and introverted blocks between which are located the various living spaces. But the theme in the proper sense is provided by a composition by Bela Bartók which makes use of the musical device of the "*stretto*," in which four movements alternate with complementary qualities. From this, and from a drawing by Paul Klee developed out of a musical stave, the house gradually derives its dualisms, and above all the one between rectangular and curvilinear geometries. One of his most fascinating concept sketches prescribes the proportions: 45 percent of chance ordering and 55 percent of mathematical ordering. Each component of the building belongs to a world: that of the spatial dams, that of the skipping roofs, and that of the aqueous spaces.

23

Concept sketch for Stretto House, Dallas, Texas 1989-1991.

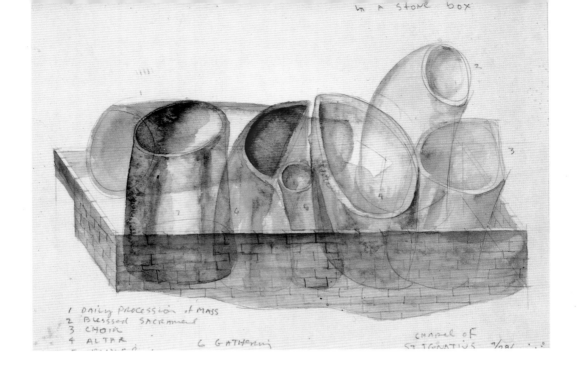

In a stone box

1 DAILY PROCESSION of MASS
2 BLESSED SACRAMENT
3 CHOIR
4 ALTAR
6 GATHERING

CHAPEL of
ST. IGNATIUS

Bottles of Light,
watercolor, concept
diagram for
St. Ignatius Chapel,
Seattle University,
Washington
1994-1997

In an interview, Steven Holl has called these conceptual diagrams his "secret weapon." In *Parallax* he provided a concise definition of them that relates back to that of *Intertwining*: "Concepts, the tools one uses to drive design, transcend ideological arguments. We work from a limited concept, unique for each site and circumstance. The limited concept gives us the freedom to work within the contingent and the uncertain. It is a strategy designed to raise architecture's expression to a level of thought. Limited concepts aim at a fusion: instead of a philosophy about architecture, they lead to an architecture that embodies philosophy." (S. Holl, *Parallax*, cit., p. 346). There are three works that can be read in light of these statements. It is a reading that should be made above all against the projects and buildings, and their most evident and immediate way of functioning, trying not to let oneself be influenced by the author's sketches and concise texts, which have also been reproduced in this volume.

The St. Ignatius Chapel at Seattle University is based on the image of seven bottles of light, later reduced to five in the built work. One aspect to which little attention has been paid until now is the regularity of the figure in which the elaborate composition of the roofs is effected. The large pan-

In the sketch:

MIT STRATEGY "HOUSES" OF INDIVIDUATION,
  – UNIQUE TYPES & CHARACTERS (spirit)
  – POUROUS OPENINGS = VIEWS TO RIVER
    FROM other side of TRACKS
  – COMMON Activities @ street level for
    Activation — 2 the LIGHT (parking below)
  – UPPER TERRACES w/ RIVER VIEWS

100' (A)

(B)

(C)

POUROUS

els that form the perimeter look more like the filling-in of a section than the walls of pavilions fused together. A dialectic between regular outline and internal complexity exists in several projects, including the Bellevue Museum. It affirms the respect of an urban order, justifying the amputation of the volumes, which reflect instead the relations within the space. This tension can be found in the church, where it exists between the hierarchy of the spaces in plan and the variety of the roofing volumes, which do not coincide schematically. In fact, the volumes must respond to another agenda: that of light. To obtain the desired effect inside the church and in the context of the campus, it was necessary to invent a complex mechanism that is not immediately apparent from observation of the technical drawings of the sections. Between the inside and the outside there are in succession: the glazing; a colored lens; a backdrop of a different color; and a second detached wall that reflects the light onto the plaster of the interior, scored to make it react more strongly to grazing light.

The second project to be considered is the recently built dormitory for MIT. In this case, the concept adopted is porosity, and the metaphor that of a sponge. The first incarnation of this porosity is urban in character. The suc-

Concept sketch for Simmons Hall, MIT, Cambridge, Massachusetts 1999.

MIT Sponge,
concept sketch for
Simmons Hall,
MIT, Cambridge,
Massachusetts 1999.

Facing and
following page,
concept sketches
for the extension to
the Nelson-Atkins
Museum of Art,
Kansas City,
Missouri 1999.

cession of four buildings that constituted the masterplan proposal was intended to encourage passage from both sides of the campus by means of the gaps between them, as well as through them. The scheme responds to strictly urban concerns, but the four buildings in turn present themselves as idiosyncratic personalities in their own right. Each has its own individuality, due to singular typological experiments that confirm the totemic character to which reference has already been made.

Some have seen this aspect as the first problematic element in a building that is proving to be controversial, but it is probably an irreversible condition, one which will not permit Steven Holl and many other architects to make a return to architectural anonymity. Other degrees of porosity are gradually proposed: the indentation of the building lets large quantities of empty space pass through its compactness. And finally the dense and deep-set pattern of the facade in structural concrete bestows a permeable appearance on the shell. But the real surprise lies in the large organic cavities that explicitly refer to the image of the sponge and brutally hollow out the regular and uniform mass of the construction. These dual-function spaces (as meeting places and lungs of the natural ventilation system) stop at the plane of the facade and are cut off by it. This confirms once again a design device that seems to turn the Abbé Laugier's maxim on its head: turmoil in the details, great order in the whole.

The third and last project to be analyzed is the expansion of the Nelson Atkins Museum. In recent years, dozens of museums have planned extensions, making them a truly recurrent theme. One must acknowledge that Steven Holl's project calls into question the accepted practice of setting a new block next to an existing one with more or less tact, or with a polemical spirit of juxtaposition. At first sight, what he is proposing is just a new landscape. The existing neoclassical building is assigned the nature of stone, the expansion that of feather. In reality the organism that is placed alongside the museum stretches to the maximum length compatible with circulation to envelope the old structure, in a way that is not initially perceptible. As previously pointed out in connection with the St. Ignatius Chapel, the relationship between, above (the lenses), and below (the circuit of the rooms) is not perfectly coincident and this helps to create a positive tension between circula-

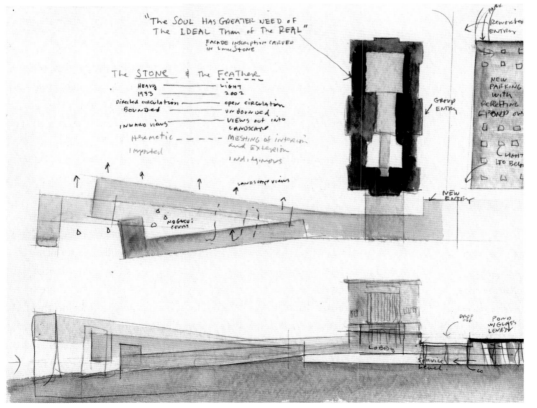

"The SOUL HAS GREATER NEED of
The IDEAL Than of The REAL"

FACADE INSCRIPTION CARVED
IN LIMESTONE

The STONE & The FEATHER

HEAVY	LIGHT
1933	2002
DIRECTED CIRCULATION	OPEN CIRCULATION
BOUNDED	UNBOUNDED
INWARD VIEWS	VIEWS OUT INTO LANDSCAPE
HERMETIC – – – –	MESHING of INTERIOR and EXTERIOR
Imported	Indigenous

LANDSCAPE VIEWS

NOGUCHI COURT

PARK

REWORKED ENTRY

NEW PARKING WITH REFLECTING POND ON

LIGHT TO BELOW

GROUP ENTRY

NEW ENTRY

LOBBY

DROP OFF

POND W/ GLASS LENS

SERVICE LEVEL

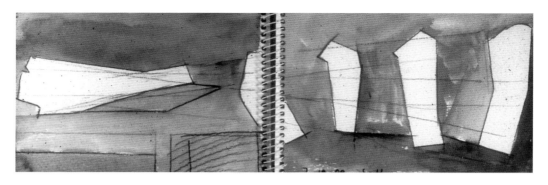

tion and internal spaces. Above, the sketches and the models recount the exciting process of perfecting luminous objects on the basis of proportions and folds that attain a sculptural refinement. Below, the sequence of rooms adapts to it, but this is redressed by the different systems used to let light penetrate from above, as well as by the opening onto the parterre that enables visitors to re-orient themselves. History, represented by the old museum, is observed and respected, but not experienced—perhaps just marvelously framed. In fact, the new entrance is located in the first lens, the wing that flanks the old museum to form a courtyard flooded with water.

These last three projects are complementary from the point of view of their respective programs: a church, a dormitory, a museum. However, contemporary practice tends to reduce the value of these differences to just one ingredient among others in the production of architecture. This last is, in Steven Holl's words, an abstract journey: "The path of passage in architecture must lead from the abstract to the concrete, the unformed to the formed. While a painter or a composer might move from concrete to abstract, the architect must travel in the other direction, gradually incorporating human activities in what began as an abstract diagram." (S. Holl, *Parallax*, cit., p. 345).

In Steven Holl's concept sketches, the genesis of the project is revealed with a clarity that is full of poetry. In the design process a form takes shape that remains more difficult to explain, lying beyond the path precisely indicated by the architect. In reality, what is deployed here is an art of composition (revealed for example by the countless study models) which remains central for him, notwithstanding the numerous challenges arising from the claim that technology has changed the ontological conditions of architecture.

Production and Reproduction

Steven Holl has a critical and conscious relationship with the contradictions created by the mode of existence of today's architecture. He began working in the seventies (when the antagonism of some architects seemed doomed to be confined to the drawing board), and since that time has decided to act within these contradictions. One of these which is fundamental, besets the production of architecture. When an architect crosses the threshold of success, and the sites of his or her projects are scattered all over the world, it is no longer possible to make use of the lessons of earlier periods. Today the practice of architecture requires an enormous amount of time devoted to coordination, administration, the drafting of plans and documents, and supervision. All this exceeds the capacities of the individual creator/author, whom everyone expects to remain at the center of the opus. So expounding a theory, making clear the link between a constant *modus operandi* and the variety of the circumstances, becomes an indispensable tool. The leading figures in architecture are all wrestling with this problem and in some cases the difficulties they encounter are plain to see. Steven Holl places between himself—solitary author—and the collective work, an ethos, a way of thinking, a rigorous poetic world. Finally, in addition to the problem of production, there is that of reproduction. For the global architectural community, the works whose photographs can be seen in this book exist chiefly on pages like these. Only one reader in a thousand is actually able to experience the material consistency—of maybe one out of ten buildings—to which their designer devotes so much attention. Steven Holl laments this: "Today publications on architecture are particularly problematic. For example, if you consider space and color, both of these can be severely distorted from a wide-angle lens, with color distortion from film and filters. Transparent colors are difficult to photograph." (J. Pallasmaa, "Thought, Matter and Experience [a conversation with Steven Holl]," cit., p. 27). Once again this problem is mitigated by a system of protection that the author has forged as a system of thought. Yet it is not judged as such. We are not interested in the opinion of a philosopher on the appropriateness of the reading of Merleau-Ponty: its litmus test is the productivity in the project. The works collected in this volume represent a substantial corpus that can be appreciated even without the laborious critical exercise of this long introduction, to which would be preferable the experience of a visit.

POOL HOUSE AND SCULPTURE STUDIO

SCARSDALE, NEW YORK, USA, 1981

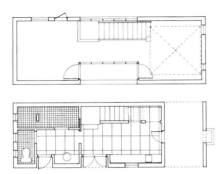

A sculpture studio and a bathhouse are sited next to an existing swimming pool. The bathhouse provides both a changing and refreshment area near the pool. The sculpture studio is situated adjacent to the bathhouse to enable it to function occasionally as a guest room.

The site in Scarsdale, New York has a history that dates from the transference of property rights by King George in the early eighteenth century. The land is marked by stone walls that were used to define its boundaries.

The project is organized with the idea of walls within walls. New walls enclosing the existing pool form a courtyard recalling the ancient stone boundary wall around the site. On the north wall of the new court, the pool house and sculpture studio form a two-story pavilion. The sculpture studio on the upper level receives light from two major windows and a pyramid skylight, which also marks the major axes on the site. Construction is of insulation-filled concrete block with smooth plaster interiors and luminous gray stucco exteriors. Red integral-color concrete pavers in the courtyard provide contrast with the dark green marble of the details and countertops. The floor of the bathhouse is flesh-colored marble. The white ceramic tile of the shower room is broken by a green marble water column with brass shower fixtures. Glass openings in the lower doors have sandblasted drawings carved in them that relate to the history of the site and the architectonic ideas.

Top, ground-floor plan, second-floor plan.
Facing page, view of the house and plan of the lot with garden.

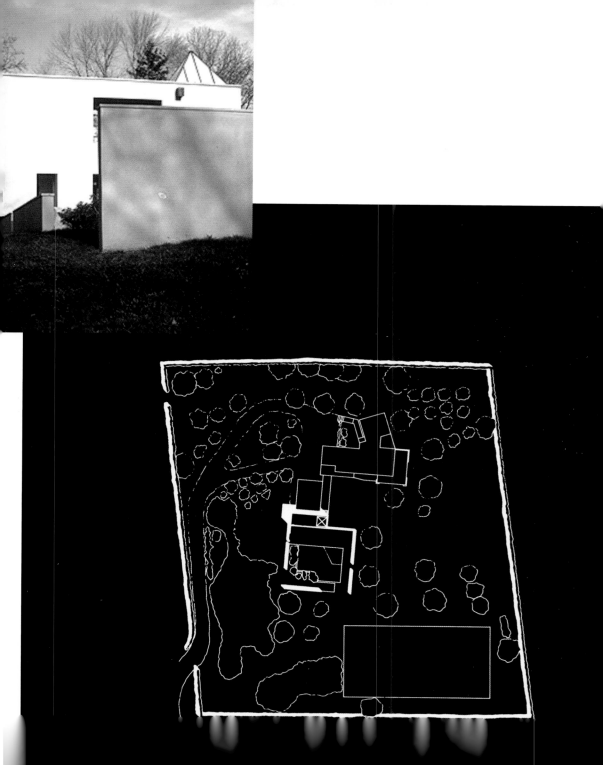

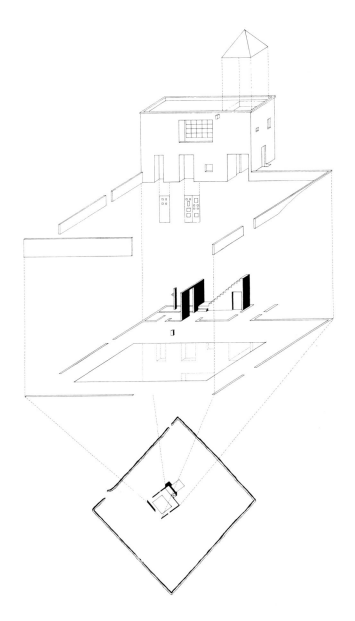

Above, exploded axonometric projection of the house.

Facing page, view of the house showing the garden and swimming pool.

BERKOWITZ-ODGIS HOUSE
MARTHA'S VINEYARD, MASSACHUSETTS, USA, 1984-1988

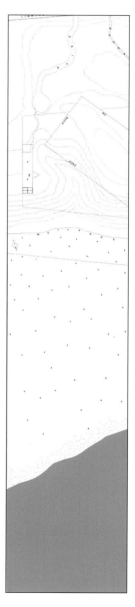

The site is a hill overlooking the Atlantic Ocean as it meets Vineyard Sound. A strict planning code determines that the house must be set back from the marshland as well as from a no-build zone on a hill and that it should have a one story elevation when viewed from the beach. Also the code stipulates that the house must be built in a natural weathered grey color wood.

In the locally inspired novel Moby Dick, Melville describes an Indian tribe, which made a unique type of dwelling on the island. Finding a beached whale skeleton, they would pull it up to dry land and stretch skins or bark over it, transforming it into a house.

This house is like an inside-out balloon frame structure. The wooden bone-like of the frame carry an encircling veranda, which affords several ocean views. Along this porch, wood members could receive the natural vines of the island. The ground vine tendrils transform the straight linear mode of the architecture.

Top, view of the house; right, site plan.
Facing page, view of the porch.

The plan is a simple set of rooms set perpendicular to the view within the setback lines of the site. Beginning with a mud and recreation room off the entry, there are two bedrooms, a kitchen and a dining room in a protective bay. The living room drops down according to the site. The master bedroom on the second level has a special view to the ocean across an exercise and sun deck on top of the main house. The wood frame with 6 in. × 6 in. vertical members is treated and exposed to weather. The 2 in. × 2 in. wood members of the guard railings as well as the 3/4 in. × 8 in. board siding is weathered wood. Windows are insulated glass in painted wood frames. The fireplace is of locally gathered stones set in concrete.

Top, views of the porch and the living room.
Facing page, exploded axonometric projection and watercolor.

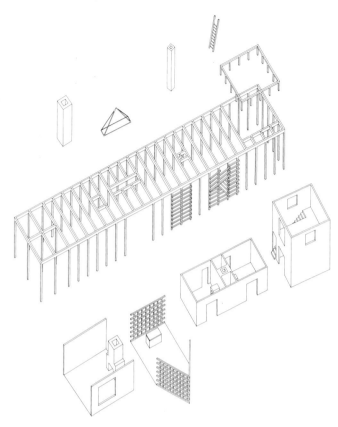

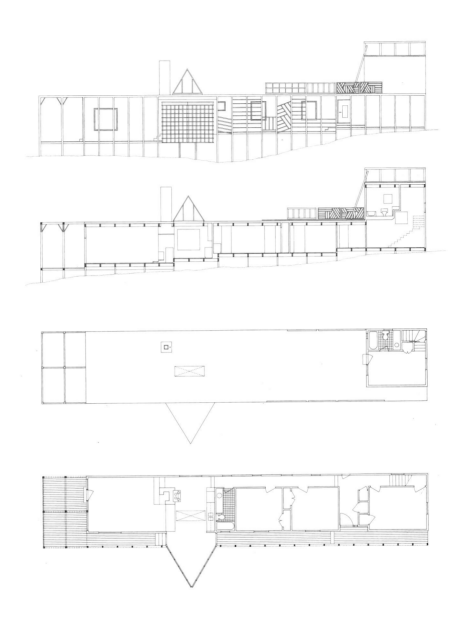

From top to bottom, southeast elevation, longitudinal section, ground-floor and second-floor plan.
Facing page, watercolor and view of the terrace facing onto the ocean.

Previous pages, views of the interiors.
Facing page, external view of the veranda.
Top, the porch, and internal view of the veranda.

HYBRID BUILDING
SEASIDE, FLORIDA, USA, 1984-1988

CHOCTAWHATCHEE BAY

PENSACOLA

SEASIDE

PANAMA

GULF OF MEXICO

Seaside is a new town on the Gulf of Mexico where the planners have established height restrictions, design guidelines, and easements. By their code, this project and adjoining buildings are required to form a continuous public arcade around the square.

The Hybrid building combines retail, office, and residential uses. The concentration of disjointed programs forms an incidental urbanism. Along with intensification of an urban condition, the building expresses the idea of a "society of strangers." The building forms split at the upper levels into east and west types. Those facing the setting sun and central square are rooms for boisterous types, late risers who enjoy watching the action, toasting the sunset, etc. All of their two-level flats are identical. They contain luxury bathrooms, microwave ovens, and space for parties.

Top, view of the complex from the southeast, area plan showing the location of Seaside.
Facing page, the west front with the porch.

Above, the balconies facing onto the double height of the porch.
Facing page, from top to bottom, cross section, clockwise, plans of the ground,
second, third, and fourth floor.

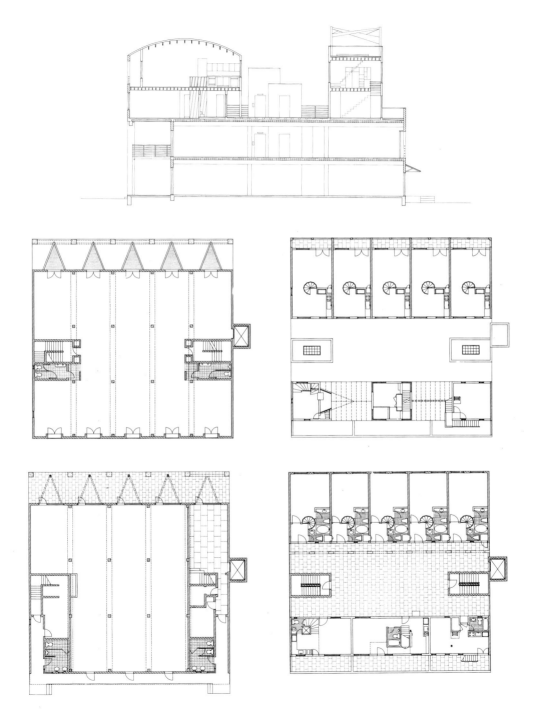

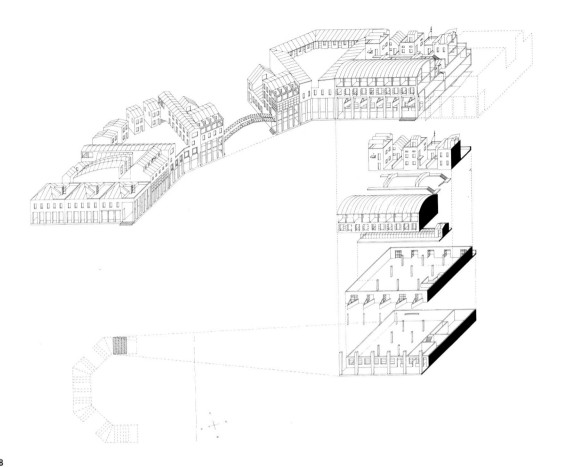

Facing east to the rising sun are rooms for melancholic types. These individuals are early risers, inclined to silence and solitude. Melancholic types are imagined as: a tragic poet, a musician, and a mathematician. The plans and sections of the three rear flats are characterized accordingly. The house of the tragic poet has a dim light; every window is of the same narrow and tall dimension. The awning at the roof is like a rag on a peasant's table. In the house of the musician, light is cast down from the corner windows on the upper level. A black plaster wall slips from the lower to the upper floor enhancing the flowing nature of the space. In the house of the mathematician everything is slightly warped. The stair to the second level warps over the bathroom. The warp over the ceiling joists forms a slight doubly-curved surface. At the second level is a calculating table with a skull shelf, in homage to Johannes Kepler.

Construction is of precast concrete columns, beams and hollow-core planks. Walls are intergral color stucco on concrete block; roofs are galvanized metal.

Top, entrance hall.
Facing page, axonometric projection of the buildings on the plaza
with axonometric exploded diagram of the hybrid building.
Following pages, view of the building from the south.

51

 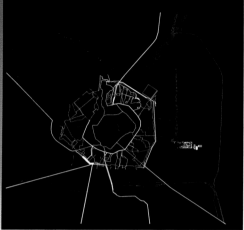

The site for this project, commissioned by the XVII Triennale of Milan, is a disused freight rail yard, bordered by blocks of housing of different types, the site fronts on to Largo Marinai d'Italia, a ragged park on land reclaimed from a poultry and vegetable market. It is in the nineteenth-century gridded portion of Milan, outside the historical center.

The program required keeping only the new "Passante" subway station, provoking the redevelopment of the area. Other functions to be located at the site included a bus station and garage for thirty buses, an air terminal station, hotels, offices, and housing. The proposal is also meant to provoke consideration of other programs for the reclamation of this metropolitan site.

The conviction behind this project is that an open work—an open future—is a source of human freedom. To investigate the uncertain, to bring out unexpected properties, to define psychological space, to allow the modern soul to emerge, to propose built configurations in the face of (and fully accepting) major social and programmatic uncertainty: this is our intention for the continuation of a "theoretical Milan."

From a dense center, Milan unfolds in circles ringed by a patchwork grid that finally sprawls raggedly into the landscape. Against this centrifugal urban sprawl (from dense core to light periphery), a reversal is proposed: light and fine-grained toward the center, heavy and volumetric toward the periphery. This proposal projects a new ring of density and intensity, adjoining the rolling green of a reconstituted landscape.

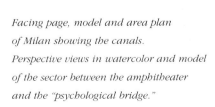

Facing page, model and area plan
of Milan showing the canals.
Perspective views in watercolor and model
of the sector between the amphitheater
and the "psychological bridge."

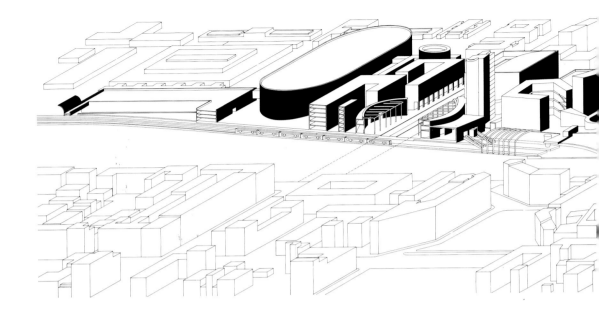

 54

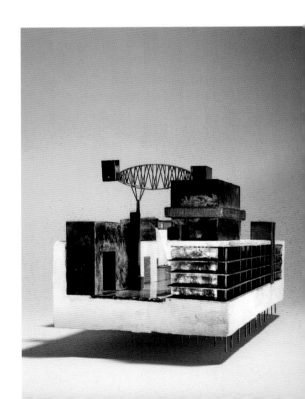

*Axonometric projection of the project
and pictures of the models.*

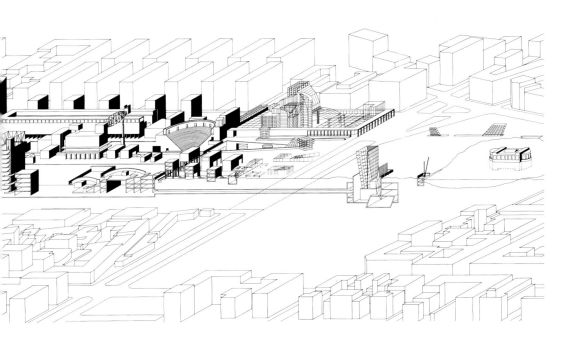

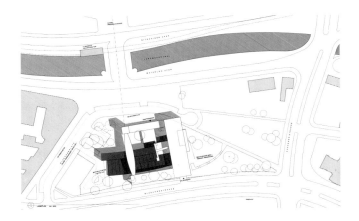

This project was awarded first prize in an invited competition for an addition to the Amerika Gedenk Bibliothek in Berlin and surrounding area.

The design extends the philosophical position of the open stack—the unobstructed meeting of the reader and the book—by organizing the offerings around a browsing circuit. The circuit is a public path looping the building, presenting the collection of the entire library. The library stacks are developed as furniture, giving different characteristics to areas of the open plan. The concept of a browsing circuit is given memorable variety by these different stack arrangements.

The circuit forms a slipped ring bracketing the original building. The extension holds the original building in space without overpowering or deferring to it. Proportions of all major architectural elements, including interior and exterior spaces and structural grid, are determined by a single series (1:1.618) based on the height of the existing building.

The importance of the site within the city plan is expressed by making the library a major urban element, analogous to a city gate. The north face of the library addition defines the south edge of the new Blucherplatz. Additional buildings to the east and west, containing public programs, complete the definition of space.

Top, area plan.

Facing page, perspective views of the reading rooms.

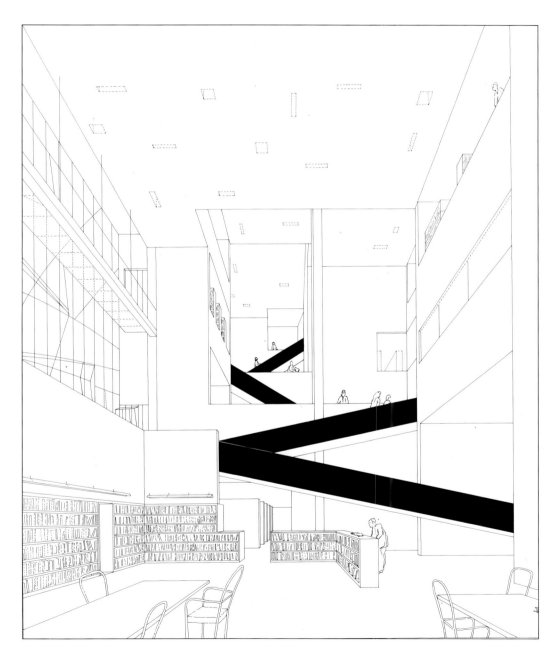

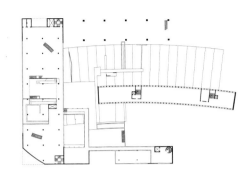

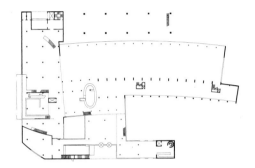

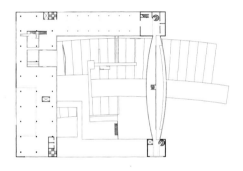

*Top, clockwise, plans of the main,
third and seventh floor.
Right, perspective view of the reading rooms.
Facing page, from top to bottom, sections
through the main block, the children's
library and the bridge that spans
the existing building.*

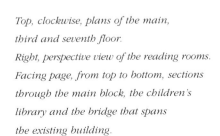

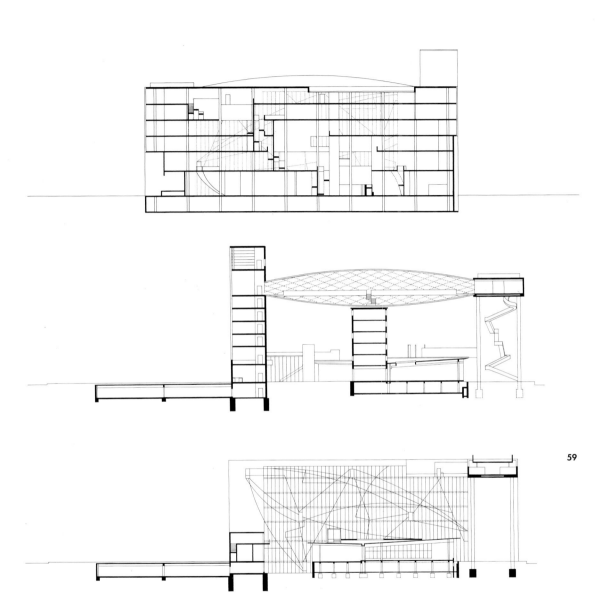

A clearly defined public park to the east and west strengthens the connection to the Holy Cross Church.

The tower offers a public observation point – a lens focused on the city – and supports the children's library.

Pictures of
the model.

Suspended over the original building, the library elevates children to caretakers of the city. It has sloped floors for reading while lying down. The structure is a lattice truss sheathed in sandblasted glass with vision panels.

The main structure is an exposed concrete frame with glass curtain walls of sand-blasted white, amber, and blue glass set off by areas of lead or stainless-steel covered panels. Under the grey skies of Berlin, the effects of east and west light in the library will be highly varied according to the sandblasted lines and mullion patterns in the curtain walls. For the interior, careful attention has been given to acoustics to assure silence, while natural materials and subdued colors have been selected for their contributions to a serene and reflective mood.

SPATIAL RETAINING BARS

PHOENIX, ARIZONA, USA, 1989

The most prominent aspect of the history of Phoenix is the mysterious disappearance of the Hohokum Indian civilization after 1000 years of continuous cultivation of the Valley with 250 miles of 30 foot canals.

Sited on the periphery of Phoenix, a series of spatial retaining bars infer an edge to the city, a beginning to the desert. Each structure inscribes a 180 degree space while rising to frame views of the distant mountains and desert.

The loft-like living areas in the upper arms hang in silent isolation forming a new horizon with views of the desert sunrise and sunset. Communal life is encouraged by entrance and exit through courtyards at grade. Work is conducted electronically from loft-spaces adjoining dwellings. Cultural facilities are suspended in open frame structures.

The 30 ft × 30 ft building sections act as reinforced concrete hollow beams. Exteriors are of pigmented concrete with the undersides of the arms polished to a high gloss. In the morning and evening these undersides are illuminated by the red desert sun; a hanging apparition of light once reflected by the water of Hohokum canals.

Top, nighttime view of Phoenix, area plan showing the contact between the urban fabric and the bars.
Facing page, plan of the city showing the spatial retaining bars at the edges.

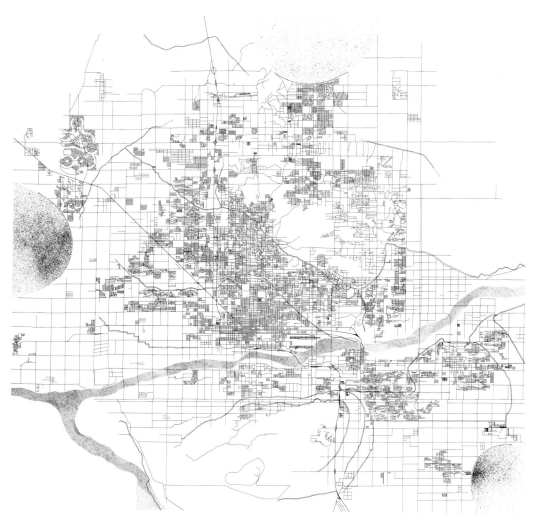

63

Facing page, axonometric projection and photomontage.

Top, model of one of the bars showing the internal distribution of the apartments.

SPIROID SECTORS
DALLAS/FORTH WORTH, TEXAS, USA, 1990

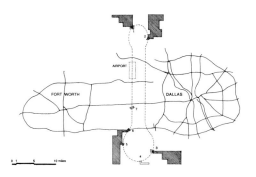

Protected Texas Prairie is framed by new sectors condensing living, working and recreation activities. Future inhabitants are delivered auto-free by high-speed MAGLEV transit from the Dallas-Fort Worth Airport in minutes.

A new hierarchy of public spaces is framed by the armatures which are knotted in a continuous holding together morphology. Various public passages along the roof afford a shifting ground plane invigorating the interconnected experience of the sector's spaces.

The looping armatures contain a hybrid of macro programs; public transit stations, health clubs, cinemas, and galleries, with horizontal and vertical interconnected transit. Micro-programs of domestic activities are in smaller adjacent structures. The smallest spiroids form low-cost courtyard housing in experimental thin/thick wall construction.

Top, diagram of the cities of Dallas and Fort Worth, connected by the monorail
that also links the spiroid sectors.
Facing page, photomontage.

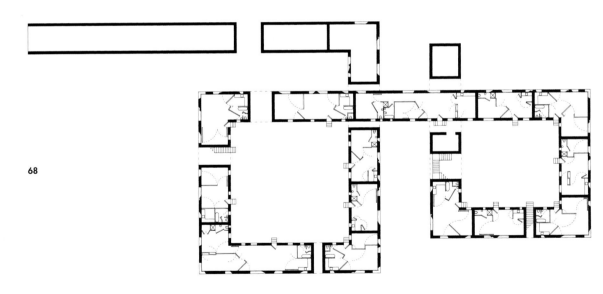

Top, view of the model; bottom, plan of the temporary apartments.

Facing page, views of the model of one sector of the housing, and of the general model.

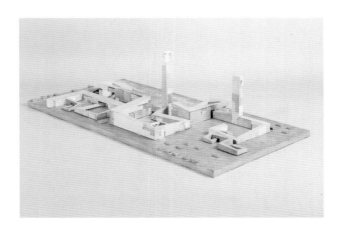

STRETTO HOUSE
DALLAS, TEXAS, USA, 1989-1991

Sited adjacent to three spring-fed ponds with existing concrete dams, the house projects the character of the site in a series of concrete block "spatial dams" with a metal framed "aqueous space" flowing through them. Flowing over the dams, like the overlapping stretto in music, water is an overlapping reflection of the space of the landscape outside as well as the virtual overlapping of the spaces inside.

A particular music with this "*stretto*," Bartók's *Music for Strings, Percussion and Celeste* was a parallel on which the house form was made. In four movements, the piece has distinct division between heavy (percussion) and light (strings). Where music has a materiality in instrumentation and sound this architecture attempts an analogue in light and space, that is

$$\frac{\text{material} \times \text{sound}}{\text{time}} = \frac{\text{material} \times \text{light}}{\text{space}}$$

The building is formed in four sections, each consisting of two modes: heavy orthogonal masonry and light and curvilinear metal. The concrete block and metal re-

Top, view of the southeast front, site plan.
Facing page, detail of the front opening onto the living room.

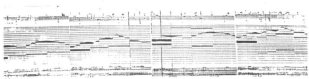

call Texas vernacular. The plan is purely orthogonal, while the section is curvilinear. The guest house is an inversion with the plan curvilinear and section orthogonal, similar to the inversions of the subject in the first movement of the Bartók score. In the main house aqueous space is developed by several means: floor planes pull the level of one space through to the next, roof planes pull space over walls and an arched wall pulls light down from a skylight. Materials and details continue the spatial concepts in poured concrete, glass cast in fluid shapes, slumped glass and liquid terrazzo.

Arriving at the space via a driveway bridging over the stream, a visitor passes through overlapping spaces of the house, glimpsing the flanking gardens arriving at an empty room flooded by the existing pond. The room, doubling its space in reflection, opening both to the site and the house, becomes the asymmetrical center of two sequences of aqueous space: arriving finally at an empty flooded room.

73

Left, view of the entrance.
Top, parallel between the form of the house and a drawing by Klee.

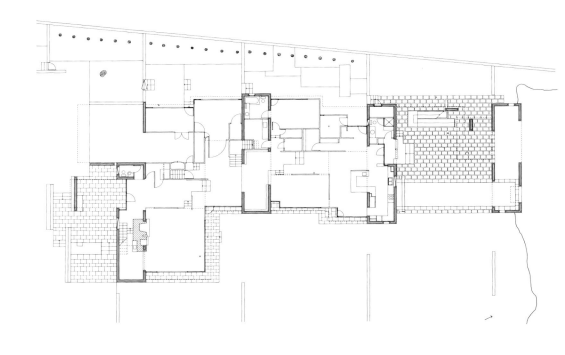

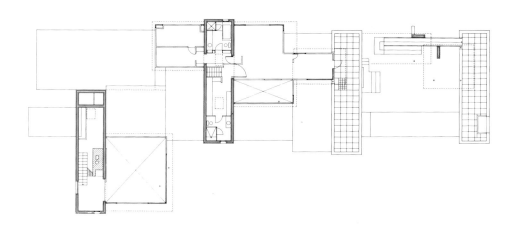

74

Facing page, plans of the ground floor and second floor.
Above, the ramp that leads to the belvedere at one end of the house;
below, longitudinal section.

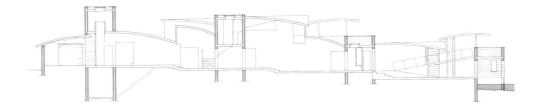

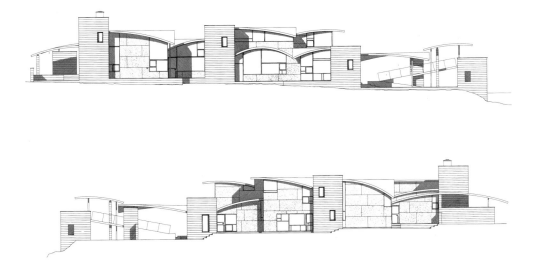

Facing page, top, view of the courtyard; bottom, east and west elevations.
Top, detail of the interior.

FUKUOKA HOUSING
FUKUOKA, JAPAN, 1989-1991

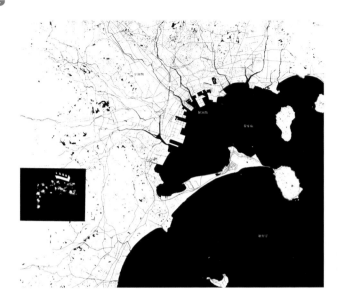

From hinged space to the silence of void space. Four active north facing voids interlock with four quiet south facing voids to bring a sense of the sacred into direct contact with everyday domestic life. To ensure emptiness, the south voids are flooded with water; the sun makes flickering reflections across the ceilings of the north courts and apartment interiors.

Interiors of the twenty-eight apartments revolve around the concept of "hinged space," a development of the multi-use concepts of traditional Fusuma taken into an entirely modern dimension. One type of hinging, diurnal, allows an expansion of the living area during the day, reclaimed for bedrooms at night. Another type, episodic, reflects the change in a family over time: rooms can be added or subtracted to accomodate grown-up children leaving the family or elderly parents moving in.

An experiential sense of passage through space is heightened in the three types of access, which allow apartments to have exterior front doors. On the lower passage, views across the water court and through the north voids activate the walk spatially from side to side. Along the north passage one has a sense of suspension with the park in the distance. The top passage has a sky view under direct sunlight.

Top, plan of the city showing the location of the project.
Facing page, view of the north front.

Top, views of the south front from the road.
Facing page, the space of one
of the courtyards.

The apartments interlock in section like a complex Chinese box. Individuation from the standpoint of the individual inhabitant has an aim in making all twenty-eight apartments different. Due to the voids and interlocking section, each apartment has many exposures: north, south, east, and west.

The structure of exposed bearing concrete is stained in some places. A lightweight aluminum curtain wall allows a reading of the building section while walking from east to west along the street; an entirely different facade of solids is exposed walking from west to east.

The building, with its street-aligned shops and intentionally simple facades, is seen as part of a city in its effort to form space rather than become an architecture of object. Space is its medium, from urban to private, hinged space.

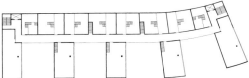

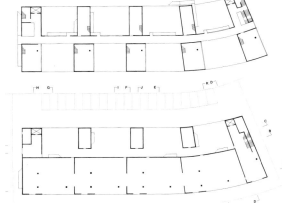

Left, from bottom to top, plans from the ground to the fifth floor and section. Facing page, diagram showing the eighteen variants of the five types of apartment: L-shaped, I-shaped, D-shaped (on two stories) and the two combinations, DI and DL.

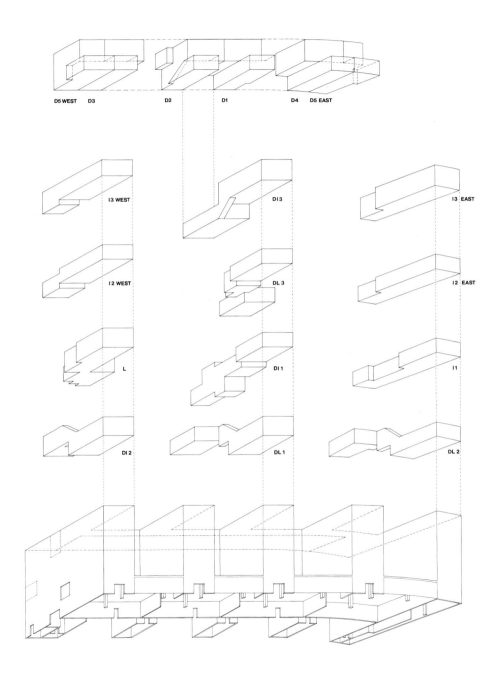

D5 WEST   D3   D2   D1   D4   D5 EAST

I3 WEST   DI3   I3 EAST

I2 WEST   DL 3   I2 EAST

L   DI 1   I1

DI 2   DL 1   DL 2

83

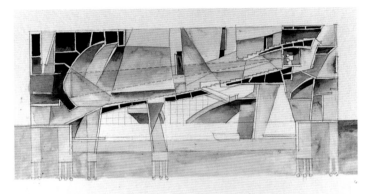

The connection of the Lido site to Venice by water is emphasized by a grand arrival of space on the lagoon. Filled with diaphanous light from gaps between the cinemas above this space—an homage to Venice—would also be a place for the Lido community. During the months when there is no cinema festival, this public grotto might have shops along the arcade or marina functions allowed to coexist with the Palazzo del Cinema.

Time in its various abstractions link architecture and cinema. The project involves three interpretations of time and light in space:

1) Collapsed and extended time within cinema is expressed in the warp and extended weave of the building, analogous to cinema's ability to compress (20 years into 1 minute) or extend (4 seconds into 20 minutes).

2) Diaphanous time is reflected in sunlight dropping through fissure space between the cinemas into the lagoon basin below. Ripples of water and reflected sunlight animate the grand public grotto.

3) Absolute time is measured in a projected beam of sunlight which moves across the "cubic pantheon" in the lobby.

The projection of light in space, light in reflection, and light in shade and shadow are seen as program to be achieved parallel to solving functional aspects.

A vessel for "filmic time" and "filmic space," the building perimeter is bottle-shaped with the mouth open to the lagoon towards Venice. The cinemas interlock within this frame, creating essential crevices and fissures which allow sunlight to the water below. In section, like interlocking hands, the cinemas turn slightly, changing their interior and exterior aspects of space.

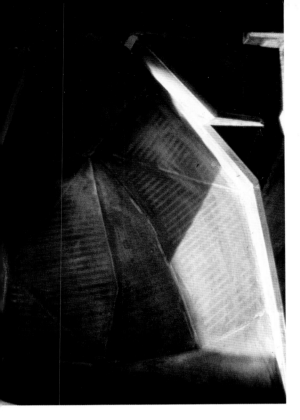

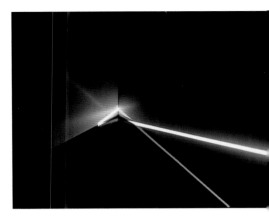

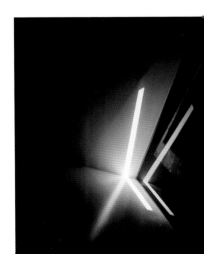

Facing page, section of the project in watercolor and area plan.
Studies of the behavior of light in the models of the "cubic
pantheon" and of one of the rooms.

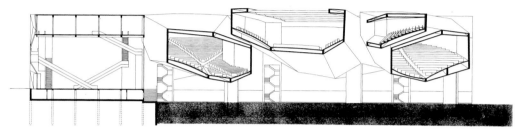

Bottom, plan at the level of the entrance to the cinemas.

Top, perspective view in watercolor and longitudinal section.

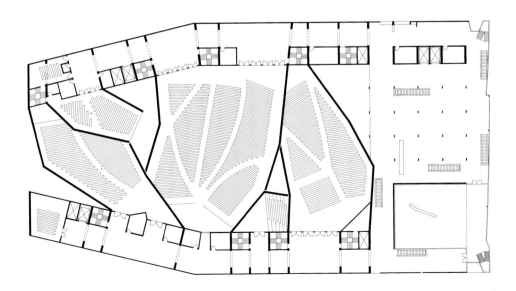

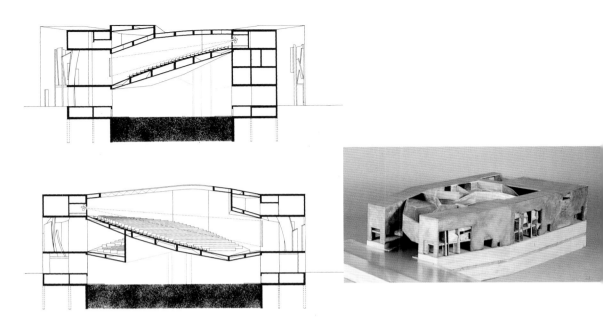

Top, cross sections and photo of the model; bottom, plan at street level.

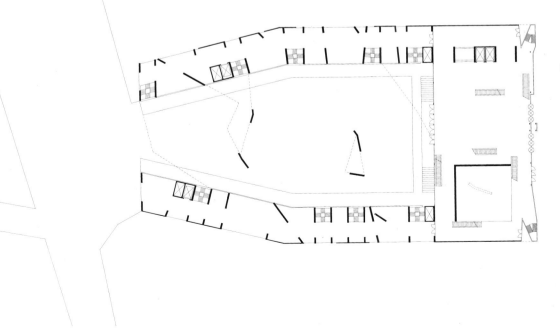

87

NEW YORK, NEW YORK, USA, 1992-1993

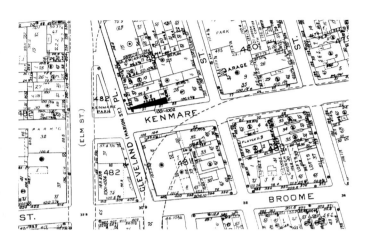

In 1992, Steven Holl and artist Vito Acconci were commissioned as a collaborative team to renovate the aging facade of the Storefront for Art and Architecture, one of few galleries dedicated to the exhibition of young architects in New York City. The Storefront project is the second collaborative effort by Holl and Acconci; their first work together was a 1988 urban plan for a growing arts community in downtown Washington, D.C. sponsored by the Pennsylvania Avenue Development Corporation.

The Storefront for Art and Architecture is situated on the corner of a block that marks the intersection of three distinct neighborhoods: Chinatown, Little Italy, and SOHO. The gallery itself is a limited, narrow wedge with a triangulated exhibition interior, such that the most dominant structure for the Storefront for Art and Architecture is the building's long facade. In fact, the history of exhibitions at the gallery was marked in the various cuts and layers of paint which exhibiting architects had imposed on and through this once-uniform surface.

Top, area plan showing the location of the gallery.
Right, view of the front on Kenmare Street.

The internal space with the panels open.

Drawing from this history, neither Acconci nor Holl were interested in the permanence of the facade or the idea of a static gallery space. Seeking to introduce improbability and to puncture the facade, Acconci and Holl challenged this symbolic border which underlines the exclusivity of the art world, where only those on the inside belong. Using a hybrid material comprised of concrete mixed with recycled fibers, Holl and Acconci inserted a series of hinged panels arranged in a puzzle-like configuration. When the panels are locked in their open position, the facade dissolves and the interior space of the gallery expands out on to the sidewalk. If the function of a facade is to create a division separating the inside from the outside space, this new facade, in the words of director Kyong Park, is "NO WALL, NO BARRIER, NO INSIDE, NO OUTSIDE, NO SPACE, NO BUILDING, NO PLACE, NO INSTITUTION, NO ART, NO ARCHITECTURE, NO ACCONCI, NO HOLL, NO STOREFRONT."

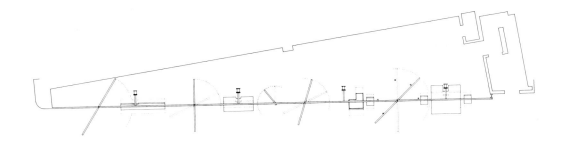

Top, plan; bottom, the front of the gallery with the panels open and closed, and detail.
Facing page, the internal space articulated by the panels.

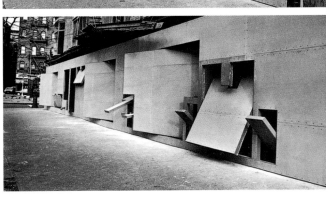

93

MAKUHARI HOUSING
CHIBA, JAPAN, 1992-1996

 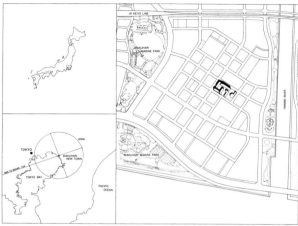

The new town of Makuhari is sited on dredged fill at the rim of Tokyo Bay. The urban planners have set rules for building height limits, tree-lined streets, areas for shops, etc. Each city block is to be designed by three or four different architects in an effort to achieve variety.

Our concept proposes the interrelation of two distinct types: silent heavyweight buildings and active lightweight structures.

The silent buildings shape the forms of urban space and passage with apartments entered via the inner garden courts. The concrete bearing wall structures have thick facades and a rhythmic repetition of openings (with variation in window or deck.) Slightly inflected, according to sunlight rules they gently bend space and passage, interrelating with movement and the lightweight structures.

Celebration of the miniature and natural phenomena are taken up in the lightweight activist force of individual characters and programs. These individuated "sounds" invade the heavyweight "silence" of the bracketing buildings. Inspired by Basho's *The Narrow Road to the Deep North*, the semi-public inner gardens and the perspectival arrangement of activist houses form an inner journey. While the interiors of apartments in the silent buildings are designed by Koichi Sone and Toshio Enomoto (Kajima Design), the exteriors of the silent buildings as well as the six activist structures are designed by Steven Holl Architects.

Top, view of the end of one of the buildings, maps showing the location of Chiba in Japan and of the block in the city. Facing page, view of the northern courtyard.

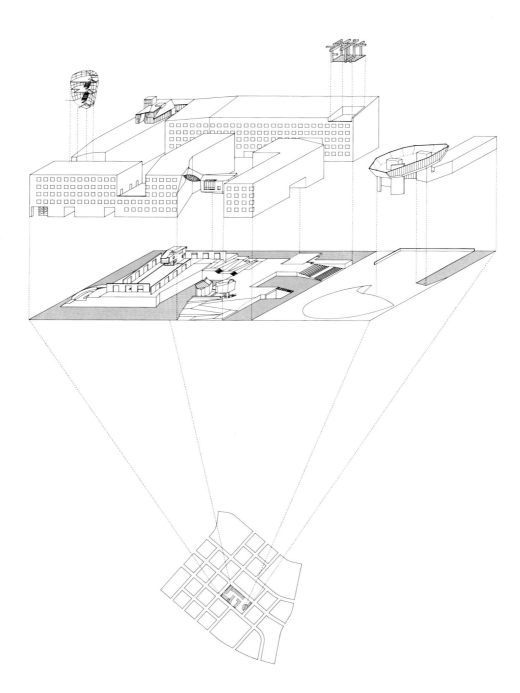

96

Above, interior of the "south courtyard house" and watercolor sketches of the south and north courtyards.
Facing page, axonometric study showing the "silent" and "militant" buildings.

Top left, the "south courtyard house,"
right, the "west courtyard house,"
bottom, the "north courtyard house."
Facing page, view of a courtyard.

"KIASMA" MUSEUM OF CONTEMPORARY ART

HELSINKI, FINLAND, 1992-1998

The site for Kiasma lies in the heart of Helsinki at the foot of the Parliament building to the west, with Eliel Saarinen's Helsinki Station to the east, and Alvar Aalto's Finlandia Hall to the north. The challenging nature of this site stems from the confluence of the various city grids, from the proximity of the monuments, and from the triangular shape that potentially opens to Töölö Bay in the distance.

The concept of Kiasma involves the building's mass intertwining with the geometry of the city and landscape which are reflected in the shape of the building. An implicit cultural line curves to link the building to Finlandia Hall while it also engages a natural line connecting to the back landscape and Töölö Bay. In the landscape plan, extending the bay up to the building will provide an area for future civic development along this tapering body of water, which also serves as a reflecting pool for Finlandia Hall and new development along the south edge of the water. The horizontal light of northern latitudes is enhanced by a waterscape that would serve as an urban mirror, thereby linking the museum to Helsinki's Töölö heart, which on a clear day, in Aalto's word's, "extends to Lapland." The changes in elevation proposed with the water extension and its shallow depth would allow for parking decks and/or highway linkages which are presently part of various planning considerations.

Top, detail of the west front, area plan showing the meeting of the lines of "culture" and "nature."
Facing page, ramp of the entrance hall.
Following pages, top, detail of the metal-clad east elevation, the building viewed from the south and, left,
the west front showing the junction between the two blocks.

This water extension from Töölö Bay intertwines with and passes through the museum. The rectangular pool along the west elevation is the source of a slow recirculating system which gradually lowers the water level. The gentle sound of moving water can be heard when walking through the cusp of the building section which remains open for passage year-round. The ponds are not intended to be drained. Instead, they are allowed to freeze in winter according to a detail first devised by Eliel Saarinen for the accommodation of the expansion of water during freezing. At night the west pond reflects the internal light radiating from the museum west pond which expresses a "spatiality of night." During the early evening hours of the winter months, glowing light escaping from the interior of the building along the west facade invites the public inside. The Helsinki Museum of Contemporary Art provides a variety

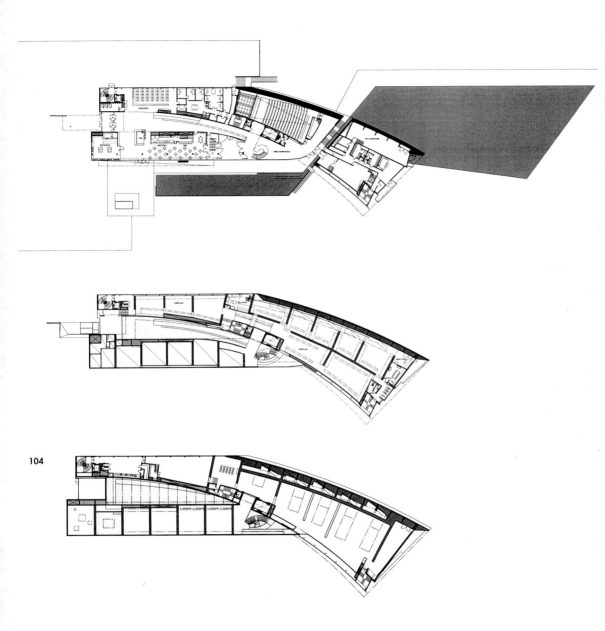

From top to bottom, plans of the ground, third and fifth floors.

Facing page, north end of the curved volume.

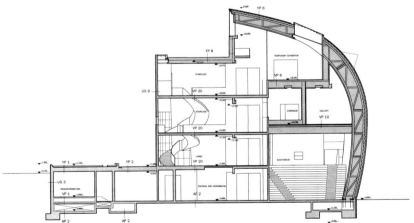

Top, one of the exhibition rooms; bottom, cross section through the auditorium.
Right, details of the skylights set in the curved façade and view of one of the exhibition rooms.

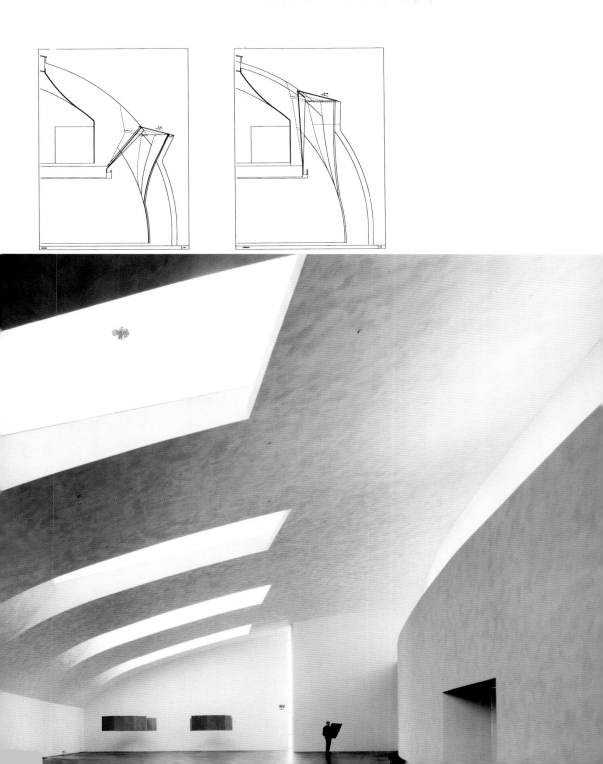

of spatial experiences. We considered the range of contemporary artwork, and tried to anticipate the needs of a variety of artists including those whose works depend on a quiet atmosphere to bring out their full intensity. These rooms are meant to be silent, but not static; they are differentiated through their irregularity.

Particular to Helsinki is the horizontal natural light of the northern latitudes. The slight variation in room shape and size due to the gently curving section of the building allows natural light to enter in several different ways. This asymmetrically drives movement through a series of spatial sequences. In this regard the overall design becomes a slightly warped gallery of rooms, where the spatial flow emerges from the combination of the horizontal light-catching section and the continuity of the internal space. This curved unfolding sequence provides elements of both mystery and surprise—which do not exist in a typical single- or double-loaded orthogonal arrangement of space. Instead, the visitor is confronted with a continuous unfolding of an infinite series of changing perspectives which connect the internal experience to the overall concept of intertwining or Kiasma.

109

Left, the spiral staircase in the entrance hall of the auditorium.
Top, view of the entrance to the museum.

CRANBROOK INSTITUTE OF SCIENCE
BLOOMFIELD HILLS, MICHIGAN, USA, 1992-1999

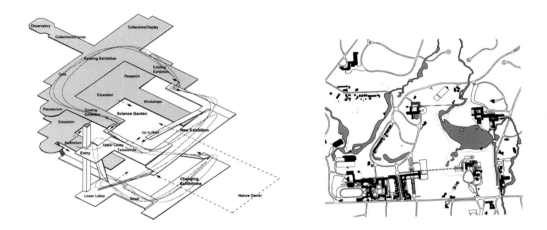

The bracketing and shaping of exterior spaces with buildings which characterizes the Cranbrook campus is continued in our addition to the Cranbrook Institute of Science. Our aim is to make the least intrusion on the architecture of the original Saarinen building while maximizing the potential for circulation and visiting experiences with the addition.

The new inner garden has a gently sloping and folding connection to the exterior campus grade. At the northwest corner the new addition passes above the ground, allowing a permeable campus grade connection which provides orientation to garden exhibits, and an open and inviting feeling.

An axis called "Stairway of Inexplicables" is formed from the new entry, roughly parallel to the existing "Ramp of the Chinese Dog." This new line of view and movement connects the Institute to existing nature trails along the sloping ground to the east.

The new addition opens up the dead end circulation of the existing 1937 galleries; the Hall of Minerals and the Hall of Man. A slipped "U" shape, like the scientific diagram for "Strange Attractors," allows for multiple paths within the exhibitions and

Top, diagram showing the interpenetration of the existing building with the new part; plan of the campus. Facing page, detail of the façade of the entrance pavilion.

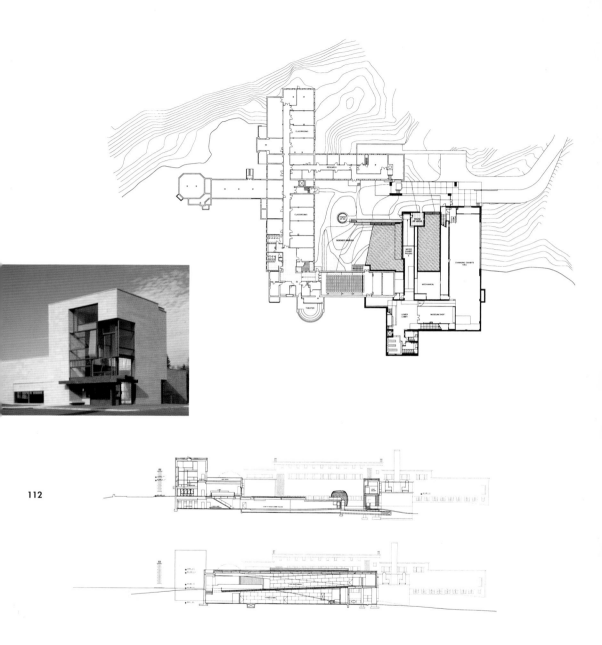

From top to bottom, plan of the ground floor with the existing building, view of the entrance pavilion and sections.
Facing page, views of the interiors and conceptual diagram of the project.

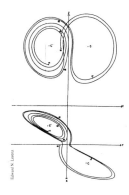

other programs of the Institute. The term "Strange Attractors" (by the meteorologist Edward Lorenz) has both geometric and experiential potential. With this concept as an analog, we aim for a free and open-ended addition which can easily adapt to change. It has unique qualities in its various circuits and routes which allow for the potential that no visit to the new science museum will be a repeat experience. Each engagement is provocative and unpredictable.

The new Institute is centered around an inner garden where scientific phenomena are exhibited in the open air. Within this "Science Garden" is the "Story of Water"; water in liquid, solid and vapor is featured in flow pools, a "House of Ice," and a "House of Vapor." Upon entering, and throughout the exhibition loops, views of the science garden orient the museum visitor.

A new entry lobby forms a "Light Laboratory" with a south-facing wall of

many types of glass. Different phenomena of light such as refraction and prismatic color are displayed on the lobby walls as the sunlight changes.

The basic structure of the addition is formed of steel truss frame spanned in pre-cast concrete planks which carry services and distribute air in their hollow cores. The exterior is clad in yellow Kasota Stone at the entry elevation, but gradually it changes to integral color concrete block on the North. The relation of stone to block is analogous to "phase space" which is a property of "Strange Attractors".

Top, the space of the "Light Laboratory" lobby.
Facing page, façade of the entrance pavilion showing the different types of glass set in the frame.

Facing page and above, effects of the "Light Laboratory" on the walls.

Facing page, the "House of Vapor."
Top, the "Story of Water"; the "Garden of Science", with the "House of Ice."

CHAPEL OF ST. IGNATIUS

SEATTLE UNIVERSITY, SEATTLE, WASHINGTON, USA, 1994-1997

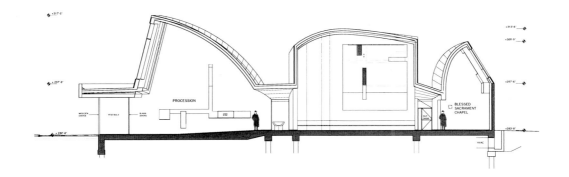

CONCEPT: A GATHERING OF DIFFERENT LIGHTS.

In the Jesuits "spiritual exercises," no single method is prescribed—"different meth-
ods helped different people...," here a unity of differences gathered into one. The
light is sculpted by a number of different volumes emerging from the roof. Each of
these irregularities aims at different qualities of light. East facing, South facing, West
and North facing, all gather together for one united ceremony.

Each light volume corresponds to a part of the program of Jesuit Catholic Worship.
The south-facing light corresponds to the procession, a fundamental part of the
mass. The city-facing north light corresponds to the Chapel of the Blessed Sacrament
and to the mission of outreach to the community. The main worship space has a
volume of east and west light. The concept of Different Lights is further developed
in the dialectic combination of a pure colored lens and a field of reflected color
within each light volume.

Facing page, the south front of the church, reflected in the pool of water.
Top, longitudinal section.

Above, plan and cross sections.

Facing page, view of part of the west front with the bell tower.

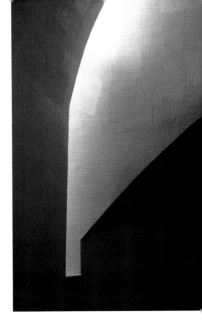

Above, the effects of the light reflected from the skylights and the sheets of colored glass.

Facing page, the nave looking toward the altar.

A baffle is constructed opposite the large window of each "bottle of light." Each of the baffles are back painted in a bright color; only the reflected color can be seen from within the chapel. This colored light pulses with life when a cloud passes over the sun. Each bottle combines the reflected color with a colored lens of the complementary color. At night, which is the particular time of gatherings for mass in this university chapel, the light volumes are like colored beacons shining in all directions out across the campus. On occasions, for those constantly praying, the lights will shine throughout the night. The visual phenomena of complementary colors can be experienced by staring at a blue rectangle and then a white surface. One will see a yel-

low rectangle; this complimentarily contributes to the two-fold merging of concept and phenomena in the chapel. The concept of "Seven Bottles of Light in a Stone Box" is further expressed through the tilt-up method of construction. The integral color tilt-up concrete slab provides a tectonic more direct and economical than stone veneer. The building's outer envelope was divided into twenty-one interlocking concrete panels cast flat on the chapel's floor slab and on the reflecting pond slab. In two days these panels were picked up and rotated into place by a hydraulic crane straining at weights up to eighty-thousand pounds. The "pick pockets," hooks inset in the panels, were capped with bronze covers once the panels were upright. Windows were formed as a result of the interlocking of the tilt-up slabs, allowing the 5/8 in. open slab joint to be resolved in an interlocking detail.

Top, the wall of the processional route; bottom, the effects of the light on the wrinkled plaster of the walls.
Facing page, detail of the hall.

*Facing page, detail of the west front
in the entrance zone.
Views of the parvis with the pool of water
and the bell tower.*

SARPHATISTRAAT
AMSTERDAM, THE NETHERLANDS, 2000

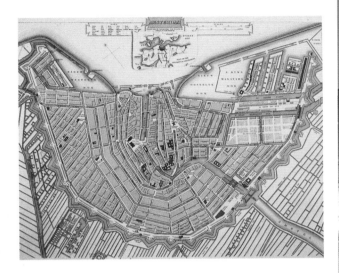

In Amsterdam, on the Singel Gracht, the renovated building is the former Federal Warehouse of Medical Supplies.

The main structure is a four-story brick "U" merging internally with a new "sponge" pavilion on the canal. While the exterior expression is one of complimentary contrast (existing brick adjacent to new perforated copper) the interior strategy is one of fusion.

The complex at 410 Sarphatistraat is entered through the original nineteenth-century brick courtyard. Passing through the interior reveals gradually more porous spaces until reaching the "Menger Sponge" pavilion overlooking the canal. While the major portion of the fifty-thousand square feet-project is workspace for the Social Housing Company's 268 employees, the large sponge space is open to receive all uses from public gatherings to performance events. Given back to the community, the immediate canal edge has a new boardwalk.

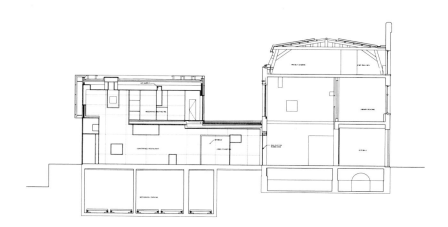

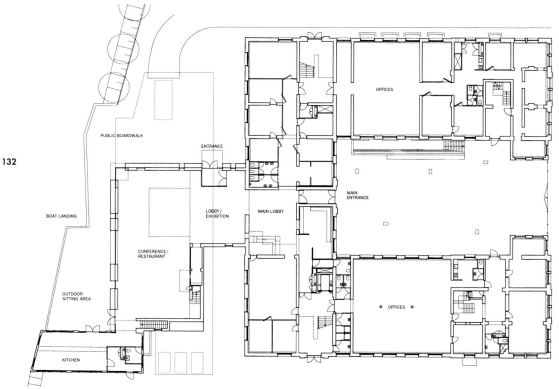

PUBLIC BOARDWALK

ENTRANCE

BOAT LANDING

LOBBY/
EXHIBITION

MAIN LOBBY

OFFICES

MAIN
ENTRANCE

CONFERENCE/
RESTAURANT

OUTDOOR
SITTING AREA

OFFICES

KITCHEN

Preceeding pages, left, plan of Amsterdam; right, the building facing onto the Singel Gracht.

Facing page, cross section and plan of the ground floor.

Above, prospect onto the double-height space; below, plan of the upper floor.

Above, model of the "Menger Sponge,"
thematic reference of the building.
Right, the space used as restaurant and
conference hall, faced with panels of sheet metal.

The porous architecture of the rectangular pavilion is inscribed with a concept from the music of Morton Feldman "Patterns in a Chromatic Field."

The ambition to achieve a space of gossamer optic phenomena with chance-located reflected color is especially effective at night when the color patches paint and reflect in the Singel Canal.

The layers of perforated materials, from copper on the exterior to plywood on the interior, contain all services such as lighting, supply and return air grilles.

The perforated screens developed in three dimensions are analogous to the "Menger Sponge" principle of openings continuously cut in planes approaching zero volume.

"Chromatic Space" is formed by light bounced between the building's layers. At night light trapped between screens sometimes appears as thick floating blocks of color. At other times the passing sun creates a throbbing color wash, or moiré patterns are created in the moving view. Below the pavilion an automatic car parking machine which takes the cars one at a time and returns them turned around is made possible on a steel framework with self-lubricating nylon wheels.

Facing page, top, the courtyard of the original building; bottom, view of the parking facility.
Above, the copper-clad building, facing onto the canal.

Facing page and above, comparison between the copper-clad extension and the brick
surfaces of the existing buildings.

KNUT HAMSUN MUSEUM

HAMARØI, NORWAY, 1996

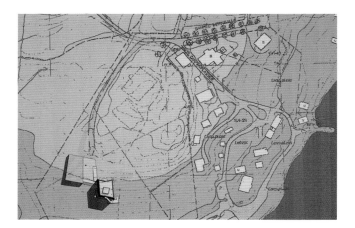

The museum will be located above the Arctic Circle near the village of Hamarøy on the farm where Knut Hamsun grew up. Knut Hamsun, Norway's most inventive twentieth-century writer, fabricated new forms of expression in his first novel *Hunger* going on in later novels such as *Pan, Mysteries* and *Growth of the Soil* to achieve the foundation of a truly modern school of fiction.

The 6458,4 square feet museum will include exhibition areas, a library and reading room, and a cafe, as well, as an auditorium equipped with the latest film projection equipment. Hamsun's writings have been particularly inspiring to filmmakers which is evident in the more than seventeen films existent. Forthcoming is a new film on Knut Hamsun, *The Enigma* by Bentein Baardson as well as one made by Swedish filmmaker, Jan Troell.

The concept for the museum is Building as a Body; battleground of invisible forces. The tarred black wood exterior skin is characteristic of the great wooden stave Norse churches. The spine of the building body is the central elevator, providing handicapped and freight access to all parts of the building. At the roof garden the long grass reflects the traditional Norwegian sod roofs in a different way.

The wood exterior is punctuated by hidden impulses which pierce through the sur-

Facing page, plan of the museum and the village. Above, photomontage.

face, such as an "empty violin case" balcony which has phenomenal sound properties and a viewing balcony which is like the "girl with sleeves rolled up polishing yellow panes." The rough white painted concrete interiors are characterized by diagonal rays of light calculated to ricochet through the section on certain days of the year.

Sited in a low field, the vertical organization allows the building to be seen from the main approach road, as well as afford magnificent views from the roof and various balconies.

The building is conceived as an archetypal and intensified compression of spirit in space and light, concretizing a Hamsun character in architectonic terms. Strange, surprising and phenomenal experiences in space perspective and light will provide an inspiring frame for the exhibitions designed by Askim and Lantto.

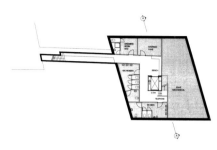

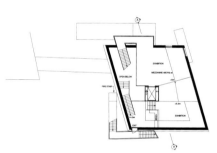

Above, photo of the model; right, plans of the basement
and second and fifth floor.
Facing page, from top to bottom, section, photo of the model
and plan of the ground floor.

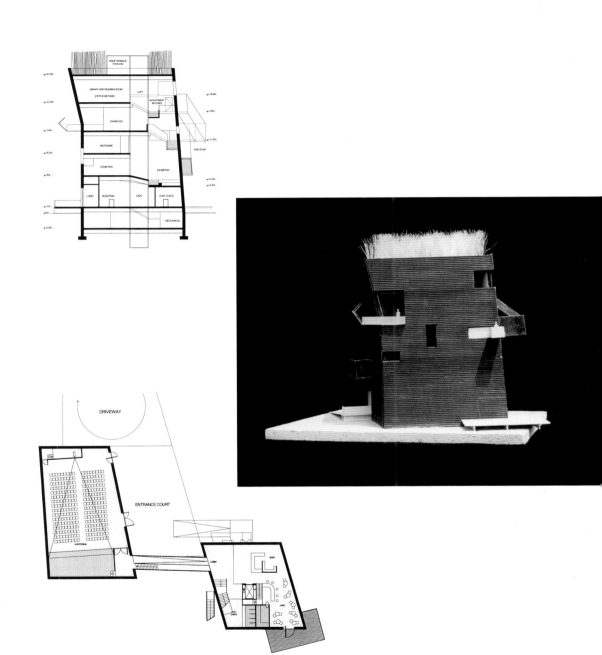

ROOF TERRACE
PAVILION

LIBRARY AND READING ROOM
(OFFICE BEYOND)   LOFT

                         (APARTMENT
                         BEYOND)

        EXHIBITION

                              FIRE STAIR

        MEZZANINE

    EXHIBITION   EXHIBITION

LOBBY   RECEPTION   CAFE   COAT CHECK

                         MECHANICAL

DRIVEWAY

AUDITORIUM

ENTRANCE COURT

                    LOBBY   SHOP

                              CAFE

                    COAT
                    CHECK

HIGGINS HALL SCHOOL OF ARCHITECTURE

PRATT INSTITUTE, BROOKLYN, NEW YORK, USA, 1997

Above, photomontage. Right, perspective view in watercolor.

PROCESS: The rebuilding of the center section of Higgins Hall presents itself after a 1996 fire. Due to a strict budget and a severely accelerated time schedule, this project might be categorized as emergency pro-architecture construction coordination.

SITE: The existing building, an "H" plan, sets the building mass in three parts with the center courts facing due west and due east. The east facing court has a fine view of the urban green rear yards in the distance. The floor plates of the existing north wing and south wing do not align. The dissonance of their difference varies increasingly in section moving vertically: on the first floors, it is 1/2 in.; on the second floors it is 1 ft. 8' in. the third floors it is 4 ft. 9 in.; on the fourth floors it is 6 ft. 7 in. Thus the dissonance moves from the detail thickness of a finger to human scale.

Rebuilding the center allows a new arrangement of program elements under the direction of the new dean, Thomas Hanrahan. For the first time the school can have a clearly oriented entrance and central entrance court. The rebuilding concept, like the building mass, is in three parts:

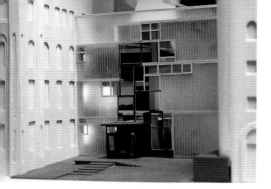

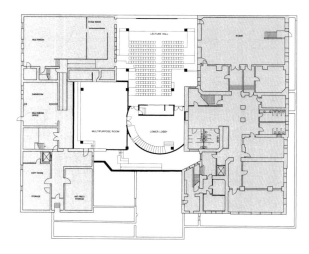

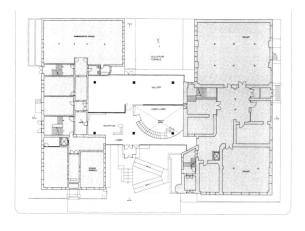

Above, photos of the model of the
entrance front from different angles;
right, plans of the basement and ground
floor, section through the building.
Facing page, plans of the second and third
floors, section between the two blocks.

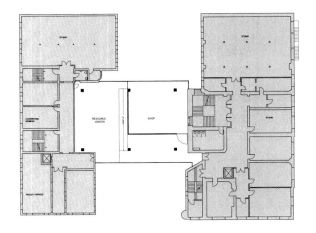

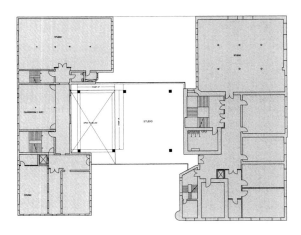

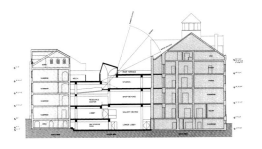

CONCEPTS:

A. The dissonance between the floor plates is opened at the center with panes of clear glass, allowing a view out at the east court and marking the new entry at the west court. A two-throated skylight marks the top, striking a dissonance of joining two types of light; south light and north light are combined analogous to harmonious sounds in a dissonant chord.

B. Brick from the burned section is recycled into a slumped brick and concrete base forming a new entrance court to the east and a viewing terrace to the west.

C. Rising out of this fire-burned brick is a concrete frame supported on six columns spanned with precast concrete planks and sheathed in a simple wall of white glass Reglit planks. An economical industrial material with translucent insulation, the planks are structural glass that span between floors, creating a translucent glow at night.

The materials for the new reconstruction are:

A. Dissonant zone: Clear glass with brass over painted steel supports.

B. Plinth: Recycled red brick and concrete.

C. Frame and Skin: White Glass translucently insulated planks, six concrete columns, precast concrete planks with integral blackened concrete topping.

147

BELLEVUE ART MUSEUM
BELLEVUE, WASHINGTON, USA, 1997-2001

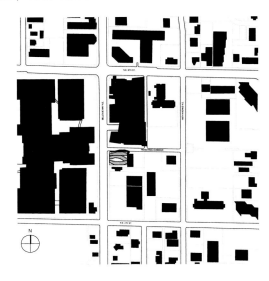

Above, area plan. Facing page, view of the building and its surroundings from the east.

The Bellevue Art Museum focuses on education and outreach rather than collecting. In fact, the museum maintains no permanent collection but rather collaborates with local arts and educational institutions to provide innovative arts programming and changing temporary exhibitions. As an "art garage" open to the street, the museum provides a new pedestrian city scale at the center of Bellevue as well as an active workshop for new art projects.

CONCEPT: Tripleness is the organizing concept for the building. A non-dialectic openness of experience, thought and contact give character to space on three levels, in three galleries, with three different light conditions and three circulation options. TRIPLENESS (non-dialectic openness): three gallery lofts; three light qualities; three actions—see/explore/make (art, science, technology); three main levels; three circulation directions.

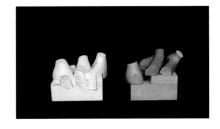

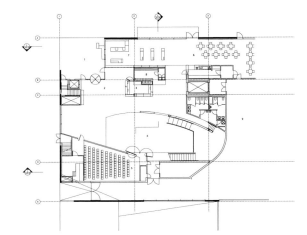

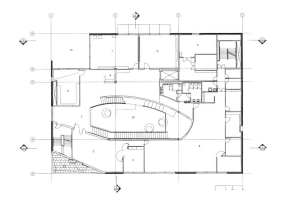

Above, watercolor sketch of the concept
of "tripleness," study models;
right, plans of the ground, second
and third floor.
Facing page, watercolor, longitudinal
and cross sections, view of the front
with the entrance.

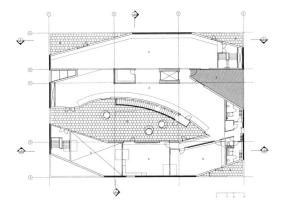

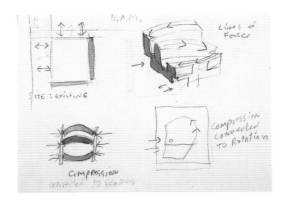

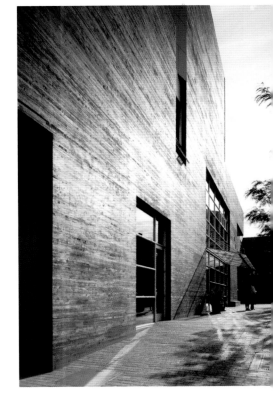

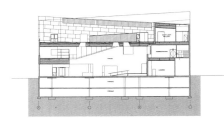

The spirit of openness of the Bellevue Art Museum is expressed in the three main lofts which are each slightly warped and gripped by the end wall structures. The outer walls in a special "shot crete" construction support the inner lightweight steel framework. The three distinct lighting conditions of the three gallery lofts are analogous to three different conditions of time and light. Linear Ongoing Time is expressed in the evenness of the light in the north loft. Cyclic Time has its parallel in the arc of south light gallery. Its plan geometry corresponds roughly to the arc of the sun at forty-eight degrees north latitude. Fragmented or Gnostic Time is reflected in the east-west skylights of the studios loft.

Above, the entrance lobby.
Facing page, an exhibition gallery and watercolors of the internal spaces.

FORUM. A stepped ramp up to the galleries pauses in a landing which double functions as a stage. Ascending to the next level one arrives at the Explore Gallery, a double-height skylit space with an adjacent artist-in-residence studio. Passing by the overlook to the Forum, the stepped ramp leads to the top level main loft galleries and the Court of Light.

Above, photo of the definitive model.

Facing page, top, the west front of the museum;

bottom, watercolor.

155

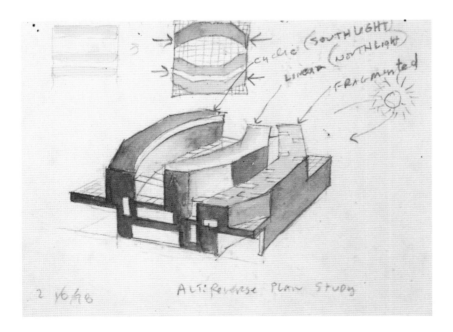

cyclic (SOUTH LIGHT)

linear (NORTH LIGHT)

FRAGMENTED

2 /6/98   ALT: Reverse Plan Study

Detail of the east front.

COLLEGE OF ARCHITECTURE
AND LANDSCAPE ARCHITECTURE

UNIVERSITY OF MINNESOTA, MINNEAPOLIS, MINNESOTA, USA, 1997-2002

Above, views of the building.
Facing page, view of the copper-clad façade from inside the lobby.

With both its interior and exterior spaces, the expansion to the College of Architecture and Landscape Architecture promotes campus activity and pedestrian circulation while providing a unified facility for the architecture and landscape architecture schools on campus.

The addition becomes a counterpoint and a complement to the existing two-hundred-foot square building with its centralized one-hundred by one-hundred feet atrium built in 1958 by Thorshov and Cerny. While the existing building is centralized and homogeneous, the new addition offers peripheral views and morphological multiplicity. The existing building is centripetal, with four right angles framing four views onto the same court; the addition is centrifugal, with four obtuse angles opening to views on four different exterior landscapes. In compliment to the horizontal facade of the existing building, the new addition has vertical elevations at the ends of each arm which stand as virtual towers, "shafts of space" activating the campus site.

The addition consists of two overlaid L-shaped masses including a new library, auditorium, seminar rooms, office and studio space. The basement and first two levels correspond with the existing building levels, and all four levels will be accessible via an elevator in the existing building.

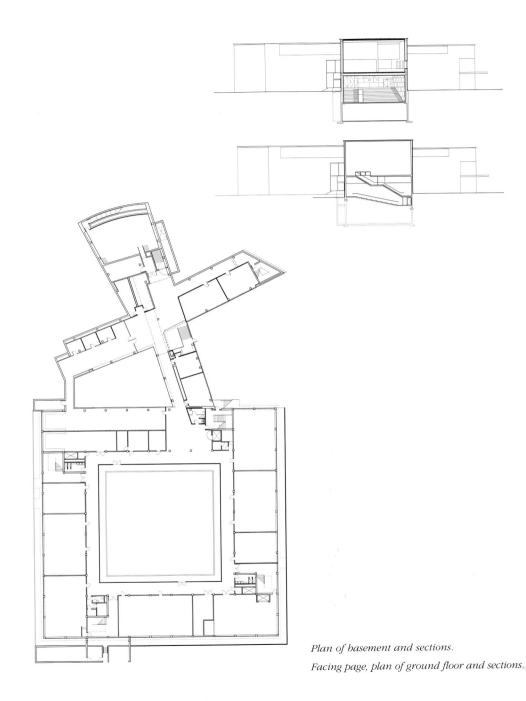

Plan of basement and sections.

Facing page, plan of ground floor and sections.

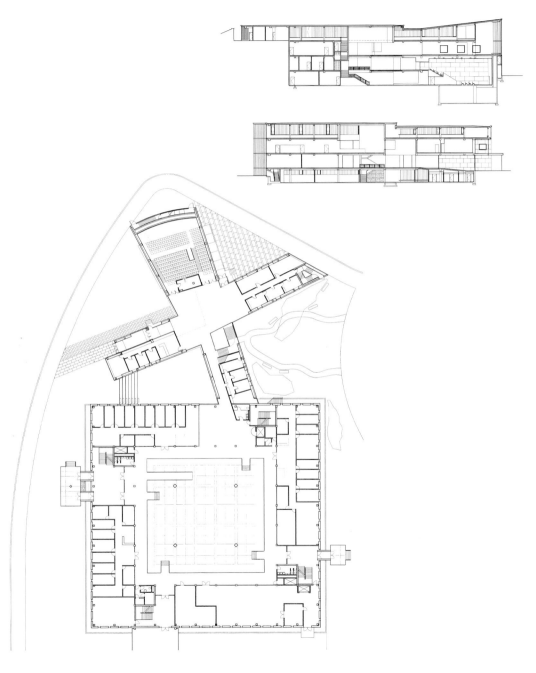

161

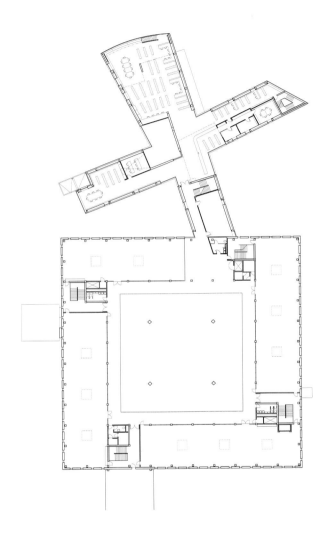

Plan of the second floor.
Facing page, from top to bottom, views of the library spaces and a lecture hall.
Following pages, the corner between two wings of the building with the entrance
on the side of the auditorium.

163

Above, the distribution space with
ceilings in exposed concrete.
Right and facing page, the library.
Following pages, the internal stairs,
constructed entirely out of reinforced
concrete.

The main entry to the west on Church Street and the entry from the Boreal Garden to the north on Pillsbury Drive both lead into a double-height central arrival space with an informal gallery and auditorium access. This dynamic center of the new addition is formed vertically in the overlap of two L-shaped voids, with a central stair leading to the library entry above. The top floor of studio space will be a large, open loft area in close proximity to the library below and studios in the adjacent existing building.

The thin plan section of each arm of the new building allows natural cross ventilation and natural light for all spaces. The addition is built with exposed precast concrete structural elements and integral color concrete floors. The horizontal inner facades are developed in naturally weathering copper with 1 in. horizontal standing seams. The soft texture of the patina green weathered copper will have the relief of shadows of the horizontal seams. During winter, strips of snow will enliven the facades with sparkling white horizontal lines.

Y HOUSE
CATSKILL MOUNTAINS, NEW YORK, USA 1997-1999

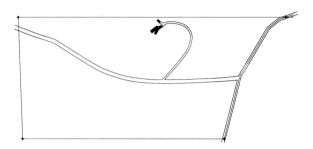

Above, site plan. Facing page, the house viewed from the west.

On a hilltop site of eleven acres with a panoramic view to the Catskill Mountains towards the South, the "Y" House continues the ascent of the hill thrust into balconies splitting into a "Y." The slow passing of time from early morning to sunset is to be a primary experience in the house as different areas of the house become activated with the movement of the sun. The geometry allows sun and shadows to "chase still time."

The "Y", like a found forked stick makes a primitive mark on the vast site extending its reaching view in several directions. The geometry of the "Y" contains a sectional flip of public/private or day/night zones. On the north half, the day zone is above and night zone below while the south half is reversed. All of these are joined in section by a central "Y" ramp.

The house occupies the hill and site through three primary relationships: "in the ground," "on the ground," and "over the ground." The portion "over the ground" suspends cantilevered above the portion "in the ground" which opens to a stone court. Various slopes of the metal roof channel rainwater to a single water cistern to the north of the house. A passive solar collection of winter sun occurs through the south glazing protected from summer sun by its deep porches.

Steel framing and steel roof are iron-oxide red, siding is red-stained cedar while interiors are white with black ash floors.

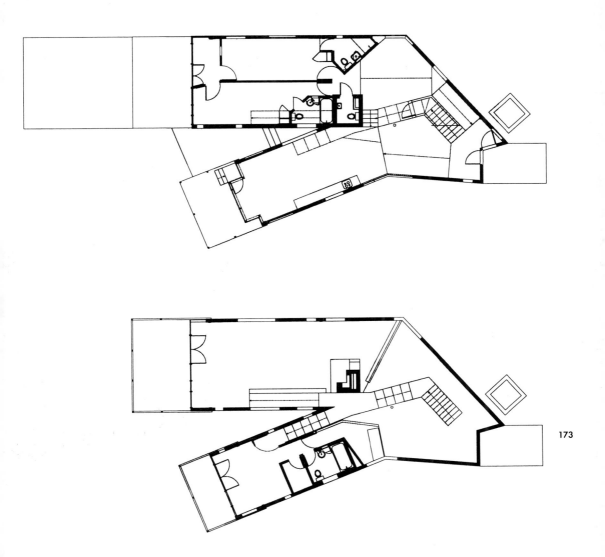

173

Facing page, detail of the metal cladding.
Above, plans of the ground and second floor.

This page, details of the west-facing terraces and of the junction between the two wings of the house. Facing page, view from the south, longitudinal and cross sections.

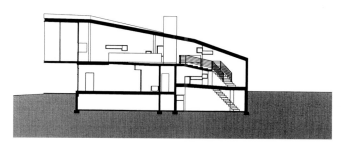

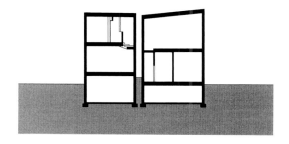

175

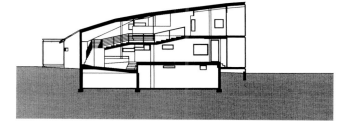

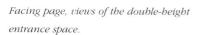

Facing page, views of the double-height entrance space.
Top, the wedge inside the house, corresponding to the junction of the two arms; bottom, the kitchen.
Following pages, the veranda facing onto the landscape and the two terraces facing west.

Above, the east front of the house. Right, the north front.

WHITNEY WATERWORKS PARK

HAMDEN, CONNECTICUT, USA, 1998

Above, area plan with the lake. Facing page, photomontage and conceptual diagram of the project. Following pages, site plan.

On the historic site of the old New Haven Treatment Plant, a new water treatment facility is being constructed. Hovering over this stainless steel tank facility is a new waterworks park. The new public park has an upper quiet-zone related to the immediate neighborhood and a more active zone related to a wider public and the Eli Whitney Museum.

The overall park is comprised of six sectors, analogs of the six basic parts of the new treatment plant below.

The new treatment facility operates at the molecular level. For example, in the ozonation portion, oxygen O_2 becomes O_3 and is bubbled through the water purifying bacterial matters. The scale change from molecular in the plant to the landscape above is celebrated in an interpretation of microscopic morphologies as landscape sectors.

GARDENS :

CHLOROPHYL GARDEN   TURBULENCE LAWN

ADMINISTRATION

MICRO TO MACRO CONCEPT

WAVE MEADOW   BUBBLING MARSH   FILTER CANOPY   WETLANDS POND

RAPID MIX

FLOCCULATION

DISSOLVED AIR FLOTATION

OZONATION

GAC FILTRATION

WATER TREATMENT PLANT :

CLEARWELL

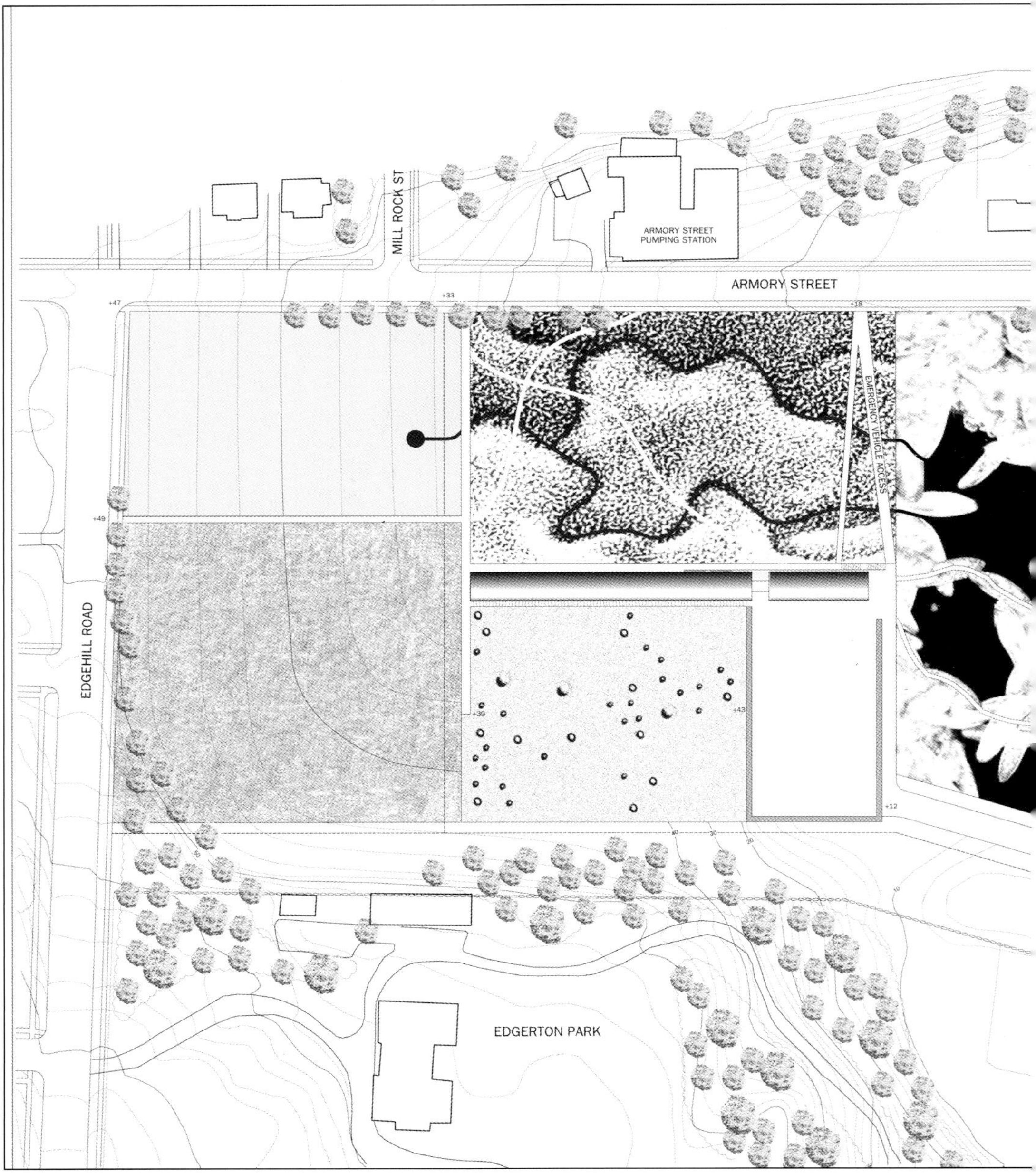

ARMORY STREET
PUMPING STATION

ARMORY STREET

MILL ROCK ST

EDGEHILL ROAD

EMERGENCY VEHICLE ACCESS

EDGERTON PARK

+47
+33
+18
+49
+39
+43
+12

LAKE WHITNEY

ELI WHITNEY
WATER
CENTER

ELI WHITNEY
BOARDING HOUSE

ELI WHITNEY
BARN

WHITNEY AVENUE

ELI WHITNEY
MUSEUM

ENTRY
TERRACE

MILL RIVER

AUDITORIUM/
COMMUNITY CENTER

PEDESTRIAN
CROSSING

ROAD

SCHEMATIC
DESIGN

185

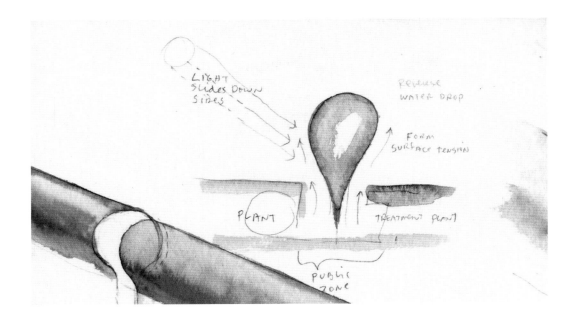

The drawing contains the following handwritten labels:

LIGHT
SLIDES DOWN
SIDES

REVERSE
WATER DROP

FORM
SURFACE TENSION

PLANT

TREATMENT PLANT

PUBLIC
ZONE

The park's "micro to macro" reinterpretation results in unexpected and challenging material spatial aspects. For example, in a field of wild mosses which corresponds to the ozonation bubbling, there are bubble skylight lenses which bring light to the plant loft below. In the zone corresponding to rapid mix and high turbulence, agitated grass mounds are penetrated by little streams.

Water flows following natural law, dropping according to gravity across the site. The turns and transformations create micro program potentials within the vast space of the new park while cleaning the water. Hints of the plant below rise up in stainless steel "slices." The administration building is formed as a stainless steel sliver rising like liquid from below. This building orients the public education entrance and is flanked by public access ways on both sides.

Facing page, watercolors of the building and the waterworks park.

Top, sketch of the internal space of the building and photo of the model from above.

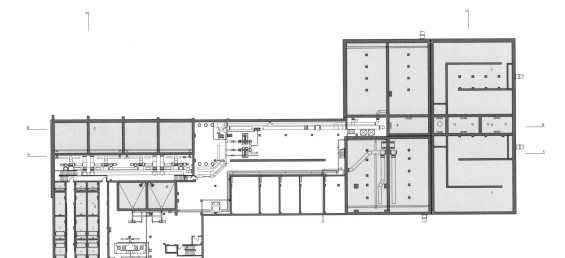

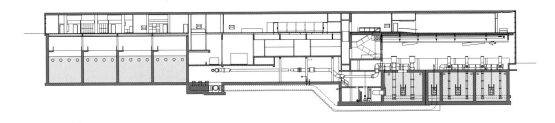

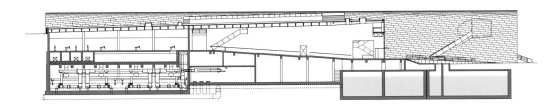

Facing page, from top to bottom, plan of the basement and
longitudinal sections through the office building and courtyard.
Top, photo of the construction site; left, photo of the model
of the office building.

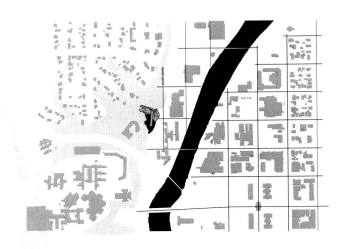

The site at the University of Iowa campus is a special condition adjacent to a lagoon and a limestone cliff. Along the Iowa River, the existing building is a brick structure with a central body and flanking wings built in 1937. The Iowa City Grid extends across the river to the limestone bluffs where it breaks up. The new building straddles these two morphologies. A 1960's addition to the school extends along the river and joins the building, covering the river-facing entrance.

A Hybrid Instrument of Open Edges and Open Center.
The new building partially bridges the lagoon and partially connects the organic geometry of the limestone bluff. Implied rather than actual volumes are outlined in the disposition of spaces. Rather than an object, the building is like a formless instrument. Flat or curved planes are slotted together or assembled with hinged sections. Flexible

Above, area plan. Facing page, photo of the model in the context of the campus.

spaces open out from studios in warm weather. The school's architecture represents a hybrid vision of the future half bridge-half loft, half theory-half practice, and half human-half scientific.

The main horizontal passages are meeting places with interior glass walls exposing on-going work in progress. The interplay of light and shadow is controlled due to the shade resulting from the overlapping planar exterior. Exposed tension rods of the partial bridge section contribute to the linear and planar architecture. The interior floors are suspended from the light capturing planar beams, which also hold the air distribution ducts and fluorescent light pockets.

Below, photo of the model with the bridge suspended above the lagoon. Facing page, top, watercolor; bottom, study models and plan of the ground floor.

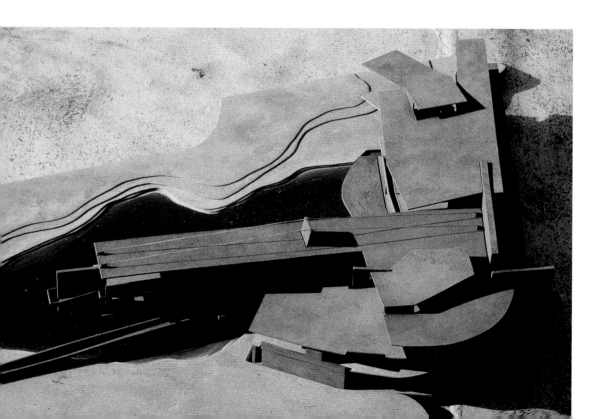

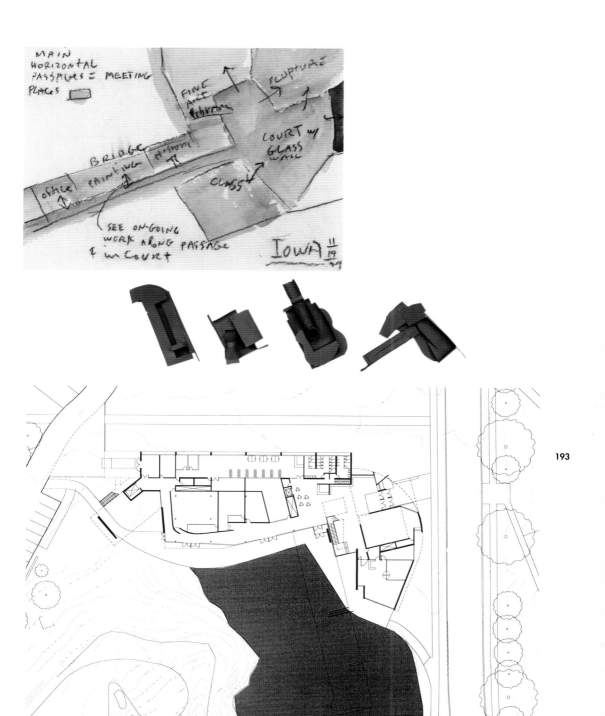

193

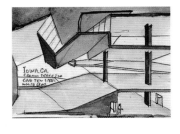

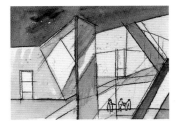

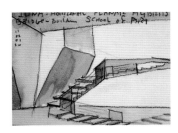

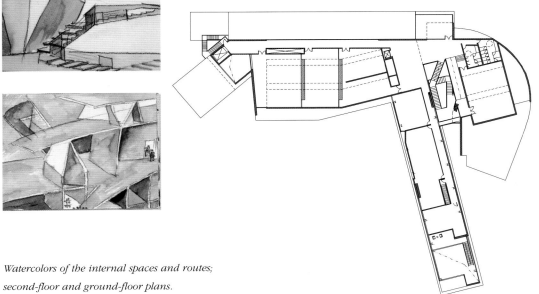

Watercolors of the internal spaces and routes;
second-floor and ground-floor plans.
Facing page, photomontages.

NELSON-ATKINS MUSEUM OF ART

KANSAS CITY, MISSOURI, USA, 1999

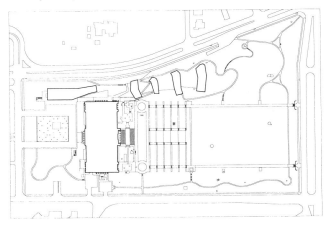

Above, site plan with the existing museum.

Facing page, photo of the model showing the light-gathering lenses next to the neoclassical building.

The expansion of the Nelson-Atkins Museum will occur through five new lenses forming new spaces, new viewpoints, and new angles of vision. From the movement of the body through the landscape and the free movement threaded between the light gathering lenses of the new addition, exhilarating new experiences of the Nelson-Atkins will be created. Glass lenses bring different qualities of light to the galleries, while the sculpture garden's pathways meander through them. Rather than an addition of a mass, we envision the new elements to be in complimentary contrast: The lenses inject light into the galleries during the day. At night the light of the galleries glows in the sculpture garden via the lenses.

A new bright and transparent glass lobby invites the public into the experiences of the Nelson-Atkins Museum. A rubber ramp escalator facilitates circulation to the continuous levels of galleries. From the lobby a new cross axis creates connection through the existing building.

At night the glowing glass of the lobby provides an inviting transparency announcing events and activities. The new parking is lit by special lenses at the bottom of the reflecting pond.

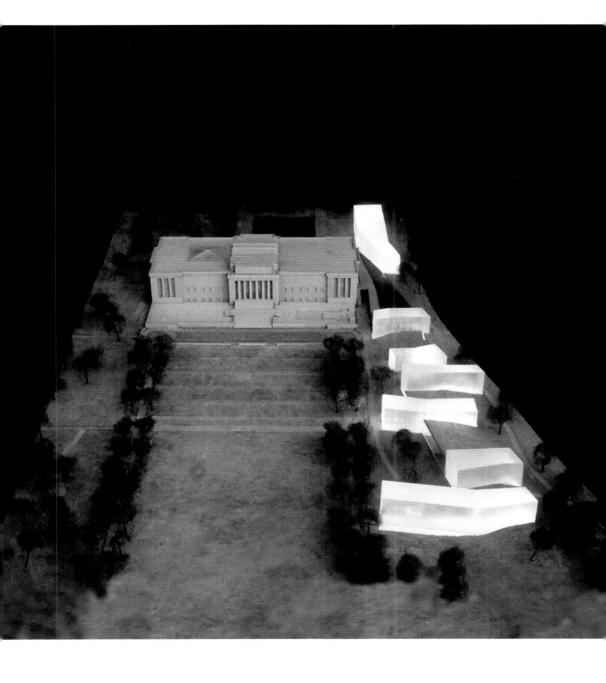

Above, photomontage; below, detail of the model at the corner of the existing building.
Facing page, picture of the construction site.

View of the pool set on top of the parking facility.
At the center of the pool, a sculpture by Walter De Maria.

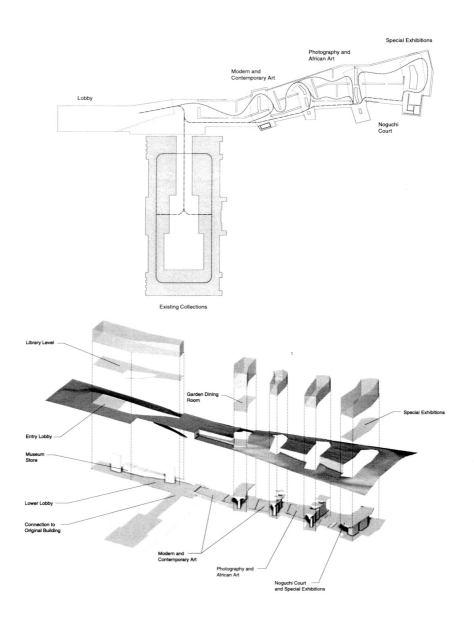

Special Exhibitions

Photography and
African Art

Modern and
Contemporary Art

Lobby

Noguchi
Court

Existing Collections

Library Level

Garden Dining
Room

Special Exhibitions

Entry Lobby

Museum
Store

Lower Lobby

Connection to
Original Building

Modern and
Contemporary Art

Photography and
African Art

Noguchi Court
and Special Exhibitions

202

*Top, scheme of the routes; bottom, exploded axonometric projection indicating the blocks
of functions.*
Facing page, top, profile facing east; bottom, the construction site (photo by Matthew Porreca).

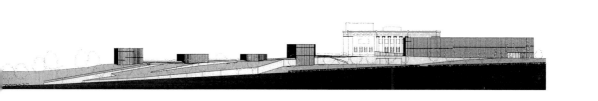

Drawings showing the relationship between architecture and landscape and concept sketch of the layout.

At the heart of the addition's glass lenses is a structural concept merged with a light and air distributor concept. "Breathing T's" bring light down into the galleries along their curved undersides while carrying the glass in suspension and providing the place for the HVAC ducts. Green building concepts include warm air plenums for gathering sun heated air and utilizing it in winter or exhausting it in summer. Computer controlled screens on south glass and special low=E materials insure the efficiency and seasonal flexibilities of the lenses structural stability is increased by slight turns in plan geometry.

All the main galleries of the addition are organized on a continuous flowing level with occasional views into the landscape of the sculpture gardens. Circulation and exhibition merge as one can look from one level to another; from inside to outside. The back and forth "meander" path in the sculpture garden above has its sinuous compliment in open flow on the continuous level of new galleries.

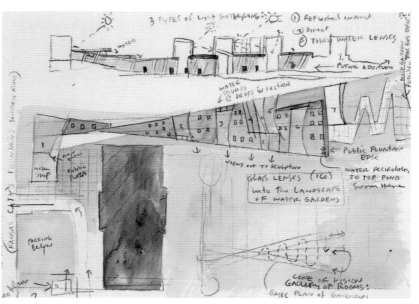

SIMMONS HALL

MIT, CAMBRIDGE, MASSACHUSETTS, USA, 1998-2002

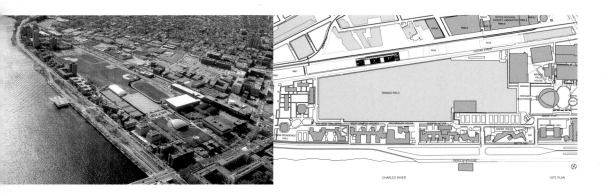

CHARLES RIVER   SITE PLAN

The three-hundredfifty-bed residence is envisioned as part of the city form and campus form with a concept of "Porosity" along Vassar Street. It is a vertical slice of a city 10 stories tall and 330 ft. long. The Urban Concept provides amenities to students within the dormitory such as a 125-seat theater, as well as a night cafe. House dining is on street level, like a street front restaurant with a special awning and outdoor tables. The corridors connecting the rooms are like streets (11 ft. wide) which happen upon urban experiences. As in Aalto's Baker House, the hallway can be more like a public place, a lounge.

CONCEPT: The Sponge concept for the new Undergraduate Residence Hall transforms a porous building morphology via a series of programmatic and bio-technical functions.

The overall building mass has five large scale openings. These roughly correspond to main entrances, view corridors, and the main outdoor activity terraces of the dormitory connected to programs such as the gymnasium.

The next scale of opening creates vertical porosity in the block with a ruled surface system freely connected to sponge prints, plan to section. These large, dynamic openings (roughly corresponding to the "houses" in the dorm) are the lungs of the building bringing natural light down and moving air up through the section.

209

Previous pages, panoramic photo and site plan, view of the south front.
Above, view of the south front.

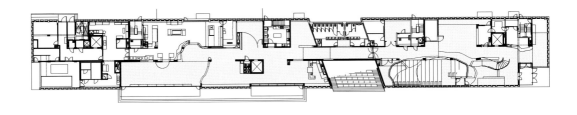

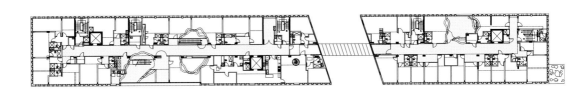

210

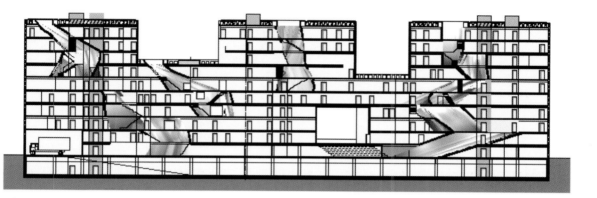

Facing page, plans of the second, third,
fourth, fifth, and sixth floors.
Top, longitudinal section; left, view of one
of the double-height common rooms
formed by the holes in the "sponge."

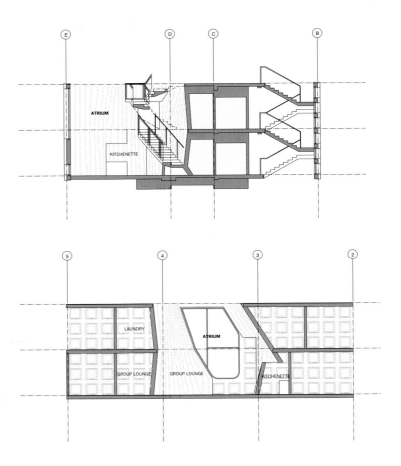

The "PerfCon" structure is a unique design, allowing for maximum flexibility and interaction. Each of the dormitory's single rooms has nine operable windows over two by two feet in size. The eighteen foot-depth of the wall naturally shades out the summer sun, while allowing the low angled winter sun in to help heat the building. In the deep setting of the numerous windows color is applied to the head and jamb creating identity for each of the ten "houses" within the overall building. The night light from the 9-window rooms will be magical and exciting.

FOUNDATION

With bedrock too deep to reach and soil too unstable to support friction piles, the building was designed to "float" like a boat in water. A volume of soil, equal to the weight of the building above, was excavated. Once complete, the pressure exerted by the building equals the pressure from the soil that had been removed. A four-foot thick solid concrete matt foundation evenly distributes the building load to the soil below.

Facing page, sections of the common spaces opened in the body of the building.
Above, Views of some of the common rooms.

INFILL WINDOWS

Computer generated structural models of the PerfCon structure showed areas that were critically overstressed due to long spans and bent spans over open corners. Select windows in these areas were filled in to resolve the overstressed conditions.

COLORED WINDOW JAMBS

Based upon a structural diagram used to coordinate the size of reinforcing steel in the PerfCon panels, the colored jambs express the anticipated maximum stresses in the structure. The colors reveal the size of the reinforcing steel cast within the PerfCon Panels. Blue=#5, Green=#6, Yellow=#7, Orange=#8, Red=#9 and #10. Uncolored areas are #5 or smaller.

NATURAL VENTILATION

Nine operable windows per single room allow students options for ventilation, views and privacy. Opening high and low windows takes advantage of the natural rise of warm air within the high-ceiling rooms.

217

Previous pages, student's room;
view of the building from the southeast.
Left, detail of the front showing
the reticular structure in concrete clad
with metal.
Top, structural diagram of the
south elevation.

Adjacent to adobe courtyard houses built by the artist Richard Tuttle, this small construction is sited atop a windy desert mesa. Its form, imagined like the tip of an iceberg indicating a much larger form below, allows turbulent wind to blow through the center. The artist's friend Kiki Smith calls it a "brooch pinned to the mesa."

The stressed skin and aluminum rib construction will be digitally prefabricated in Kansas City—then bolted together on site. P.V. cells covering the roof allow overflow power for the existing adobe constructions.

The second Turbulence House, made for an exhibition in Vicenza, Italy, for the Basilica Palladiana, will be constructed permanently in a private sculpture park in Schio, Italy.

A. Zahner and Co. is a Kansas City sheet metal fabrication company that utilizes digital definition combined with craftsmanship to produce highly intricate metal shapes and forms. By means of parametric logic, solid materials can be converted into engineered assemblies to an accuracy once considered impossible.

Facing page, watercolor.

Above, photomontage.

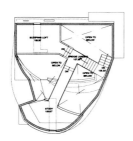

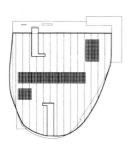

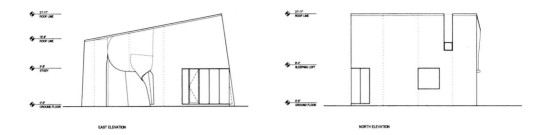

EAST ELEVATION

NORTH ELEVATION

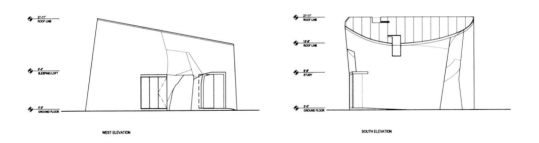

WEST ELEVATION

SOUTH ELEVATION

*Facing page, left, plans of the ground floor, second floor
and roof; right, phases in the assembly of the house on site.
Above, elevations.*

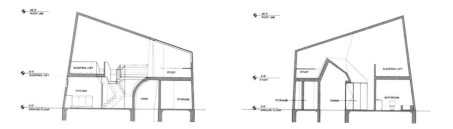

Top, the house under construction; bottom, sections.

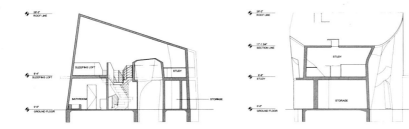

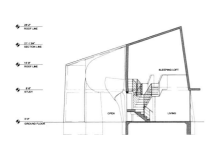

Top, the house in the snow-clad landscape, sections, and view of the construction site.

224

Above, left and facing page, reconstruction
of the house inside the Basilica Palladiana
in Vicenza on the occasion of the exhibition
on Steven Holl in September 2002.

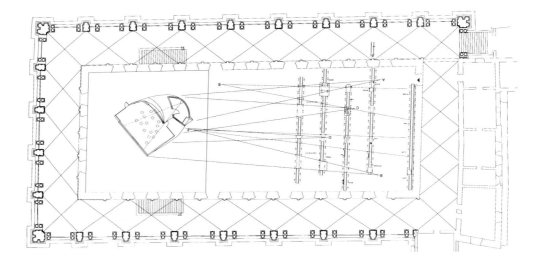

Facing page, top, plan of the Basilica with the project for the mounting of the exhibition;
bottom, the section devoted to the projects.
Top, Turbulence House, in the background of the display of the projects.

WRITING WITH LIGHT HOUSE

LONG ISLAND, NEW YORK, USA, 2002-2003

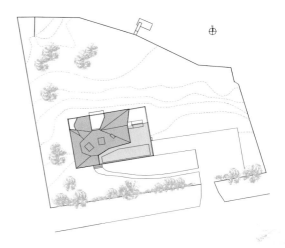

The concept of this linear wooden beach house evolved from the inspiration of the site's close proximity to the studio of the painter Jackson Pollock. Several free-form designs were made based on the 1949 painting "Seven in Eight." Opening up the interior to the free expanse of the bay and the north view of the Atlantic Ocean required closing the south side for privacy from the street.

The final scheme brackets the internal energy into an open frame, which the sun shines through in projecting lines. The strips of white light inscribe and seasonally bend internal spaces dynamically with the cycle of the day.

The wooden balloon frame construction is comparable to the strip wood sand dune fencing along the ocean. Several guest rooms swirl around the double-level living room from which one ascends to a pool suspended over the garage. From this upper pool court, the Atlantic Ocean is visible.

Top, site plan.

Facing page, top, concept sketch of the theme of "writing with light" in watercolor; bottom, photo of the model.

Concept = "WRITING WITH LIGHT"

LINEAR STRIPS of SUNLight INSCRIBE AND BEND internal SPACES DYNAMICALLY in time

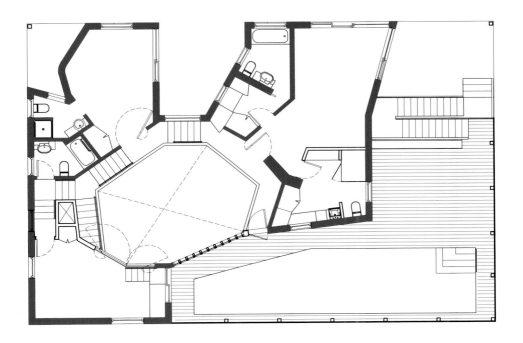

Both pages, top, plans of the ground floor and upper floor;
bottom, studies of light in the model.

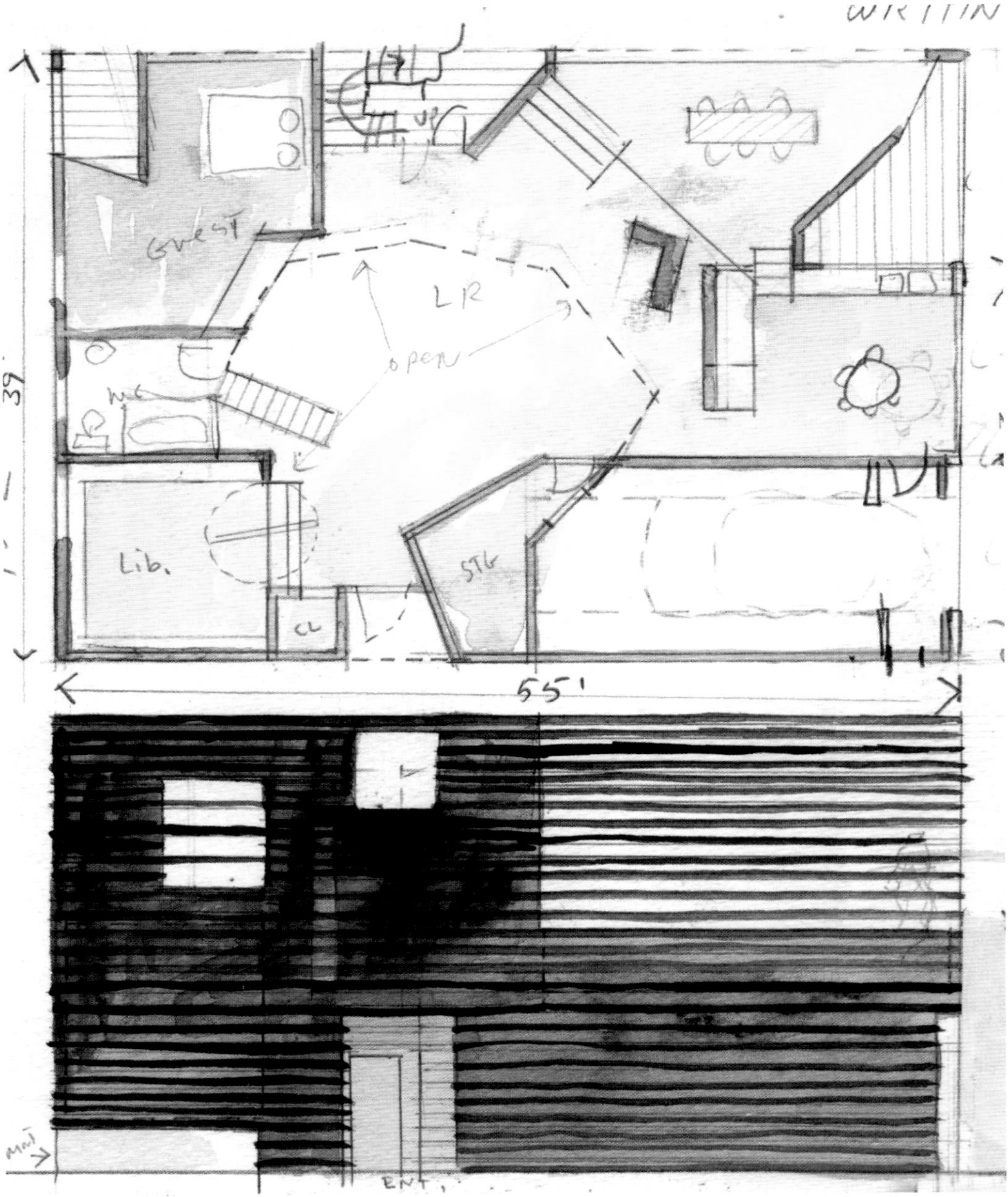

WRITIN

GUEST

LR

open

WC

Lib.

STG

CL

39

55'

232

ENT.

Mni

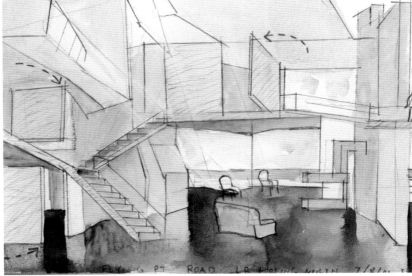

Facing page, watercolor of the disposition of masses.

Top, the model viewed from the south; bottom, watercolor of the living space.

234

Steven Holl was born in Bremerton, Washington, in 1947. After graduating from the University of Washington and a period spent studying in Rome, he did a post-graduate work at the Architectural Association in London in 1976. In the same year he opened a studio of his own in New York, Steven Holl Architects.

In 1989 the Museum of Modern Art in New York devoted an exhibition to him and to Emilio Ambasz. In 1991 his work was exhibited at the Walker Art Center in Minneapolis as part of a series entitled "Architecture Tomorrow," in a one-man show that went on to visit numerous places in America and Europe. Since then he has taken part in numerous exhibitions. The most recent were held in New York and Rome (*Parallax*, 2001), Vienna (*Idea and Phenomena*), and at the Basilica Palladiana in Vicenza, in 2002.

His work has been accompanied by a continual series of publications. In 1976 he founded the series entitled "Pamphlet Architecture," dedicated to innovative designs and theoretical research. In 1989 he published the first collection of his own projects, *Anchoring*, which was followed by *Intertwining* in 1996. His most recent books are *Parallax* (2000), *Idea and Phenomena* (2002) and the album of watercolors *Written in Water* (2002). Complete collections of his projects have been published in monographic issues of the Spanish magazine *El Croquis*, and in Italy in the Electa catalogue of 2002.

Since the mid-eighties, the works he has realized have received numerous awards, including prizes from the magazine *Progressive Architecture* and the American Institute of Architects (AIA).
In 1989 Steven Holl was appointed professor of architecture at Columbia University, where he has taught design since 1981.

Project Credits

POOL HOUSE AND SCULPTURE STUDIO

Location	Scarsdale, New York
Design year	1980
Construction year	1981
Program	Sculpture studio and bathhouse
Client	Rosen
Project team	Mark Janson, James Rosen

BERKOWITZ-ODGIS HOUSE, MARTHA'S VINEYARD

Location	Martha's Vineyard, Massachusetts
Design year	1984-1988
Construction year	1986-1988
Program	Private residence
Client	Steven Berkowitz and Janet Odgis
Project team	Stephen Cassell, Ralph Nelson, Peter Shinoda

HYBRID BUILDING

Location	Seaside, Florida
Project year	1984-1985
Construction year	1986-1988
Program	Hotel suites, shops, and offices
Client	Robert Davis
Project team	Laurie Beckerman, Stephen Cassell, Peter Lynch, Lorcan O'Herlihy, Philip Teft, Richard Warner

PORTA VITTORIA PROJECT

Location	Milan, Italy
Competition year	1986
Program	Urban planning proposal including park and botanical gardens commissioned by XVII Triennale of Milan
Client	XVII Triennale of Milan
Project team	Jacob Allerdice, Laurie Beckerman, Meta Brunzema, Stephen Cassell, Gisue Hariri, Mojgan Hariri, Paola Iacucci, Peter Lynch, Ralph Nelson, Ron Peterson, Darius Sollohub, Lynette Widder

AMERIKA GEDENK BIBLIOTHEK

Location	Berlin, Germany
Winning competition	1988
Program	Renovation and addition to the American Memorial Library
Client	Amerika Gedenk Bibliothek
Project team	Peter Lynch
Project team	Bryan Bell, Stephen Cassell, Pier Copat, Thomas Gardner, Friederike Grosspietshe, Stefan Schroth Arch.

EDGE OF A CITY: SPATIAL RETAINING BARS

Location	Phoenix, Arizona
Project year	1989-1990
Program	Proposal for a new city edge, buildings provide residential, office and cultural facilities
Project team	Pier Copat, Janet Cross, Ben Frombgen, Peter Lynch

EDGE OF A CITY : SPIROID SECTORS

Location	Dallas, Texas
Project year	1989-1990
Program	A proposal for a hybrid building type sited in the partly settled area between Dallas and Fort Worth
Project team	Laura Briggs, Janet Cross, Scott Enge, Tod Fouser, Hal Goldstein, Peter Lynch, Chris Otterbine

STRETTO HOUSE

Location	Dallas, Texas
Project year	1989-1991
Program	Private residence for art collectors
Client	Withheld at client's request
Project Architect	Adam Yarinsky
Project team	Stephen Cassell, Kent Hikida, Terry Surjan
Landscape Consultant	Kings Creek Landscaping
Structural Consultant	Datum Engineering
Mechanical Consultant	Interfield Engineering
Contractor	Thomas S. Byrne Construction

FUKUOKA HOUSING

Location	Fukuoka, Japan
Design year	1989-1991
Construction year	1991-1992
Program	Mixed use complex with 28 residential apartments
Client	Fukuoka Jisho Co.
Project team	Hideaki Ariizumi, Pier Copat

PALAZZO DEL CINEMA

Location	Venice, Italy
Competition	1990
Program	Competition for Venice Film Festival Building
Client	Venice Film Festival
Project Architect	Peter Lynch
Project team	Stephen Cassell, Janet Cross, Thomas Jenkinson, Jun Kim, Lucinda Knox, William Wilson

STOREFRONT FOR ART AND ARCHITECTURE

Location	New York, New York
Design year	1992
Construction year	1993
Program	Facade renovation for small architecture gallery
Client	Storefront for Art and Architecture
Design Architect	Steven Holl and Vito Acconci
Project team	Chris Otterbine

MAKUHARI HOUSING

Location	Chiba, Japan
Design year	1992-1995
Construction year	1995-1996
Program	190 Units of housing, retail, and public amenities
Client	Mitsui Group
Project Architect	Tomoaki Tanaka
Project team	Janet Cross, Lisina Fingerhuth, Mario Gooden, Thomas Jenkinson, Bradford Kelley, Jan Kingsbergen, Justin Korhammer, Anderson Lee, Anna Muller, Sebastian Schulze, Gundo Sohn, Terry Surjan, Sumito Takashina
Associate Architects	Kajima Design
Engineer	Kajima Design
Consultants	Konichi Sone (block design coordinator), Toshio Enomoto/Kajima Design (block architect), JUKA Garden and Architecture (landscape), L'Observatoire International (lighting)

KIASMA MUSEUM OF CONTEMPORARY ART

Location	Helsinki, Finland
Winning competition	1992
Design year	1992-1996
Construction year	1996-1998
Program	Galleries, theater, cafe, shop, artist workshop
Client	Ministry of Education, Helsinki
Project Architect	Vesa Honkonen
Project team	Tim Bade, Molly Blieden, Stephen Cassell, Pablo Castro-Estévez, Janet Cross, Justin Korhammer, Anderson Lee, Chris McVoy, Anna Müller, Justin Rüssli, Tapani Talo, Tomoaki Tanaka
Associate Architect	Juhani Pallasmaa Architects, Helsinki, Finland, Juhani Pallasmaa, Principal, Timo Kiukkola, Project Architect
Structural Engineers	Insinööritoimisto OY Matti Ollila & Co. Consulting Engineers, Helsinki
HVAC engineer	Insinööritoimisto Olof Granlund OY
Electrical Engineer	Tauno Nissinen OY Consulting Enginnering
Structural & mech. Engineers	Ove Arup & Partners, New York,
Lighting consultant	L'Observatoire International, New York
Contractor	Seicon OY, Helsinki

CRANBROOK INSTITUTE OF SCIENCE

Location	Bloomfield Hills, Michigan
Design year	1992-1995
Construction year	1996-1999
Program	Addition and renovation to existing science museum, new central science garden courtyard
Client	Cranbrook Educational Community
Project Architect	Chris McVoy
Project team	Tim Bade, Stephen Cassell, Pablo Castro-Estévez, Martin Cox, Janet Cross, Yoh Hanaoka, Bradford Kelly, Jan Kinsbergen, Justin Korhammer, Anna Müller, Tomoaki Tanaka
Structural & mech. Engineers	Ove Arup & Partners, New York, Guy Nordenson, principal in charge, Mahadev Raman, principal for MEP
Exhibit Design	Cranbrook Architecture Office
Lighting consultant	L'Observatoire International, New York
Landscape consultants	Edmund Hollander Design P.C., Cranbrook Architecture Office

CHAPEL OF ST. IGNATIUS

Location	Seattle, Washington
Project year	1994-1996
Construction year	1997
Program	Jesuit chapel for the Seattle University community
Client	Seattle University
Project Architect	Tim Bade
Project team	Jan Kinsbergen, Justin Korhammer, Audra Tuskes
Associate Architect	Olson Sundberg Architects, Seattle, WA, Rick Sundberg, Tom Kundig, Principals, James Graham, Project Manager
Structural Engineers	Datum Engineers, Houston, Monte Clark Engineering, Seattle
Mech., Elec., Plumbing	Abacus Engineered Systems, Seattle
Liturgical Consultants	Bill Brown, AIA P.C., Colorado Springs
Lighting consultant	L'Observatoire International, New York
Acoustical	Peter George and Associates, New York
General Contractor	Baugh Construction, Seattle
Artists	Linda Beaumont, Seattle. Dora Nikolova Bittau, Rome

SARPHATISTRAAT OFFICES

Location	Amsterdam, The Netherlands
Design year	1996-1998
Construction year	1999-2000
Program	Headquarters for Housing Company
Client	Woningbouwvereniging Het Oosten
Project Architect	Justin Korhammer
Project team	Hideaki Ariizumi, Martin Cox, Annette Goderbauer, Yoh Hanaoka, Heleen van Heel

Associate Architect	Rappange & Partners Architecten
Structural Engineers	Ingenieursgroep Van Rossum
Lighting Consultant	L'Observatoire International, New York
Electrical & mech. Engineer	Technical Management
Contractor	VOF Van Eesteren Koninklijke Woudenberg

KNUT HAMSUN CENTER

Location	Hamarøy, Norway
Project year	1994
Program	Historical museum for writer Knut Hamsun
Client	Knut Hamsun Center
Project Architect	Erik Langdalen
Project team	Gabriela Barman-Kramer, Yoh Hanaoka, Justin Korhammer, Anna Müller, Audra Tuskes
Associate Architect	Askim and Lantto Architects

HIGGINS HALL SCHOOL OF ARCHITECTURE

Location	Brooklyn, New York
Project year	1997-2002
Construction year	2003-2004
Program	New central wing of Pratt Institute's Architecture School
Client	Pratt Institute
Project Architect	Tim Bade
Project team	Martin Cox, Makram El-Kadi, Annette Goderbauer, Katharina Hahnle, Erik Langdalen
Associate Architect	Sclater Partners, Bradley Smith, Project Architect
Structural Engineer	Guy Nordenson and Associates (schematic design)
Structural Engineer	Skilling Ward Magnusson Barkshire, Seattle
Lighting Design	L'Observatoire International, New York
General Contractor	Sellen Construction

BELLEVUE ART MUSEUM

Location	Bellevue, Washington
Project year	1997-1999
Construction year	2000-2001
Program	Galleries, classrooms, cafe, auditorium
Client	Bellevue Art Museum
Project Architects	Tim Bade, Martin Cox
Project team	Elsa Chryssochoides, Annette Goderbauer, Yoh Hanaoka, Justin Korhammer, Jennifer Lee, Stephen O'Dell

COLLEGE OF ARCHITECTURE AND LANDSCAPE ARCHITECTURE

Location	Minneapolis, Minnesota
Project year	1997-2000
Construction year	2000-2002
Program	Addition to College of Architecture for the University of Minnesota
Client	University of Minnesota
Project Architect	Pablo Castro-Estévez, Annette Goderbauer, Katharina Hahnle
Project team	Gabriela Barman-Kramer, Molly Blieden, Yoh Hanaoka, Jennifer Lee, Rong-Hui Lin, Stephen O'Dell
Associate Architect	Vincent James Associates
Engineer	Ellerbe Becket Inc.
Structural engineers	Guy Nordenson & Assoc.
Lighting consultant	L'Observatoire International, New York

Y-HOUSE

Location	Catskills, New York
Project year	1997-1998
Construction year	1999
Program	A weekend retreat
Client	Herbert Liaunig
Project Architect	Erik Langdalen
Project team	Annette Goderbauer, Yoh Hanaoka, Brad Kelley, Justin Korhammer, Jennifer Lee, Chris McVoy
Site Architect	Peter Liaunig
Structural Engineer	Robert Sillman Associates, New York
Lighting Consultant	L'Observatoire International, New York
Contractor	Dick Dougherty,
Custom made Furniture	Face Design

WHITNEY WATERWORKS PARK

Location	Hamden, Connecticut
Project year	1998-2002
Construction year	2002-2004
Program	Public park and water treatment facility
Client	Regional Water Authority
Design Architect	Steven Holl and Chris McVoy
Associate in Charge	Anderson Lee
Project Architects	Annette Goderbauer , Arnault Biou,
Project Team	Justin Korhammer, Linda Lee, Rong-Hui Lin, Susi Sanchez, Ben Tranel, Urs Vogt
Landscape Architect	Michael Van Valkenberg & Assoc.
Engineers	CH2Mhill, Tighe and Bond Consulting Eng.

ART AND ART HISTORY BUILDING

Location	Iowa City, Iowa
Project year	1999-2002
Construction year	2003
Program	New building for the University of Iowa's Art Department. Facilities for sculpture, painting, printmaking,